ABERTILLERY
AND
EBBW VALE LINES

Vic Mitchell and Keith Smith

MP Middleton Press

Cover picture: No. 6415 is backing out of Aberbeeg station on 26th May 1956, having worked the 6.20pm autotrain from Ebbw Vale. The crew will slumber in a siding before returning up the valley. (F.Hornby)

THEY WON'T SLUMBER LONG! THE 6-20 SO WAS DUE AT
ABERBEEG AT 6.38. THE RETURN SEEMS TO HAVE
BEEN TIMED TO DEPART AT 6.42 SO!

Published August 2006

ISBN 1 904474 84 5

© Middleton Press, 2006

Design Deborah Esher
Typesetting Barbara Mitchell

Published by
> *Middleton Press*
> *Easebourne Lane*
> *Midhurst, West Sussex*
> *GU29 9AZ*

Tel: 01730 813169
Fax: 01730 812601
Email: info@middletonpress.co.uk
www.middletonpress.co.uk

Printed & bound by Biddles Ltd, Kings Lynn

If this is a southward view, and the OS map bears that out, then the ? must be <u>from</u> Sirhowy.

This is a <u>southward</u> panorama.

53 Northward

Southward (from the viaduct?).

Not somersault signals as I would know them (GN, Barry etc.). They ? standard GWR "restricted site" signals.

South eastwards.

2 Looking up the valley towards the station.

Ditto.

The train is Brynmawr bound.

Northward, not southward.

Caption means map XXX1X. From the high level bridge east of Market ? dings, looking over the skew bridge and the station.

The train has almost certainly run down from Beaufort.

Surely, the engine has already run round and now has the road down ? valley, witness the banner repeater in the "off" position.

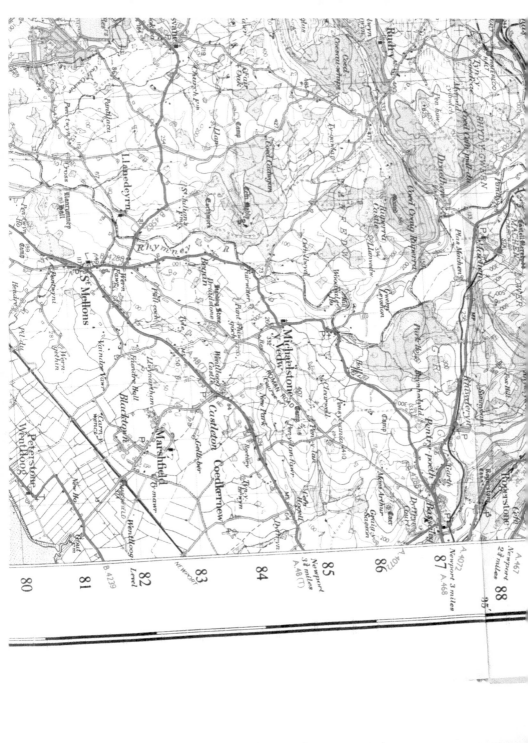

INDEX

ACKNOWLEDGEMENTS

We are grateful for the assistance received from many of those mentioned in the credits also to W.R.Burton, A.R.Carder, R.Caston, L.Crosier, G.Croughton, J.B.Horne, R.C.James, B.S.Jennings, P.J.Kelley, N.Langridge, R.Marrows, Mr and Mrs M.Miles, Mr D. and Dr S.Salter, N.Seabourne, M.Turvey, M.Vrettos, H.Williams, E.Wilmshurst and especially our ever supportive wives, Barbara Mitchell and Janet Smith.

I.   Routes in the Western Valleys in 1939.
(Railway Magazine)

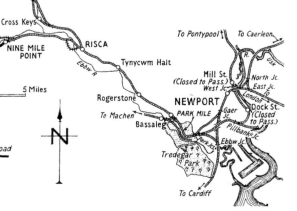

Reference:—
— L.M.S.R. (Sirhowy)
+++ Original Course of Sirhowy Tramroad
--- Other L.M.S.R. Lines
▓▓▓ G.W.R
══ Joint Lines
— Other Lines

GEOGRAPHICAL SETTING

Our route began to develop in the era of the canals in the late 18th century, when they were mainly concerned with the transport of coal and iron. Situated at the confluence of the Ebbw River and the River Usk, the docks were developed south of the wharves on the Usk and both grew greatly with the advent of the railways.

The Monmouthshire Canal ran close to the Ebbw River between Newport and Crumlin, tramroads continuing northwards in the narrowing and steepening valleys of the Ebbw Fach to Blaina and the Ebbw Fair to Ebbw Vale. These two rivers converge at Aberbeeg.

The route between Newport and Risca crosses mainly sandstone, but at the latter place it entered an area of complex geology on the eastern flank of the South Wales coalfield. The line served numerous collieries.

The maps are to the scale of 25ins to 1 mile, with north at the top, unless otherwise indicated.

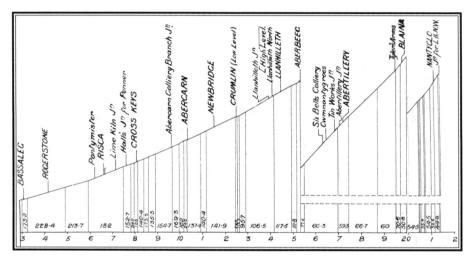

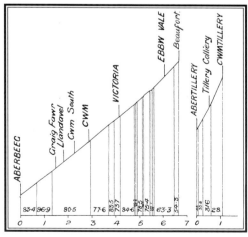

HISTORICAL BACKGROUND

The first "Rail Ways" in the area, more properly termed tramroads, were laid as extensions of the western arm of the Monmouthshire Canal, opened in 1796. A tramroad from the head of the canal at Crumlin to the Beaufort Iron Works at Ebbw Vale opened at about the same time. The Monmouthshire Canal Company was established by an Act of 1792, its name being changed to the Monmouthshire Railway & Canal Company in 1849. The MCC was empowered by an Act of 1802 to make further tramroads from Nine Mile Point (whence the Sirhowy Tramroad ran northwards to the ironworks of that name) to Newport, and Crumlin to Risca, to join that from Nine Mile Point. Where the line ran through Tredegar Park near Newport, it was built at the expense of the estate, which charged tolls for its use; this section was eventually purchased in 1923. The tramways ran to wharves on the banks of the River Usk, south of Newport. These lines opened around 1805 and were available for general goods traffic from 1811.

Other mineral lines in the area included Hall's Tramroad and the Averbeeg Tramroad. The former was completed in about 1805 and ran north from Cross Keys and crossed to the Sirhowy Valley at Pentwynmawr. The latter ran through Blaina to Brynmawr, the northern part becoming known as the Llanarth Tramroad.

Newport received broad gauge trains (7ft 0¼ ins) on 18th June 1850, when the South Wales Railway opened between Chepstow and Swansea.

The MRCC relaid its line with a combination of standard gauge/tramroad track, steam and horse traction being used between about 1830 and 1849. A timetabled passenger service started on 21st December 1850 between Newport (Court-y-Bella) and Blaina. An extension to Newport Dock Street followed on 4th April 1852 and a service between Aberbeeg and Ebbw Vale (Beaufort) began on 19th April 1852. Nantyglo was served from 16th May 1859.

Conversion of the tramroads was completed in 1855, but passenger service to the Sirhowy Valley did not begin until 1865. The MRCC had two termini in Newport; Dock Street and Mill Street, and a connection between them was completed in 1855.

Brynmawr had received trains from Abergavenny from September 1862, the service being extended to Nantybwch in March 1864. The route became part of the London & North Western Railway. It had started in 1822 as part of Bailey's Tramroad.

The Great Western Railway and the SWR were amalgamated in 1862 and broad gauge operation in the area ceased in 1872.

The MRCC became part of the GWR in 1880 and Western Valley services were transferred from

II. Map of the early tramroads. (Railway Magazine)

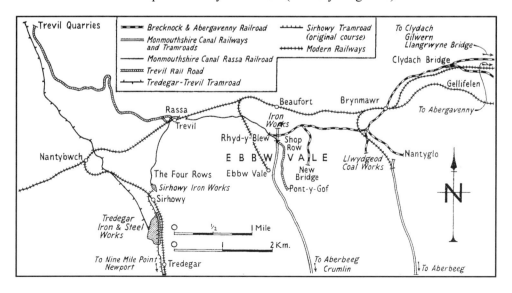

Newport Dock Street to the main line station at High Street from 1st August of that year.

A service between Brynmawr and Nantyglo began on 28th May 1906. The 1899 Brynmawr & Western Valleys Railway was jointly owned by the GWR and LNWR from 1902 and was often known as the "Missing Link".

The GWR formed the Western Region of British Railways upon nationalisation in 1948. The LNWR became a constituent of the London Midland & Scottish Railway in 1923, most of which formed the London Midland Region of BR. However, the Brynmawr-Nantyglo section became part of the Western Region.

Passenger services between Newport and Ebbw Vale, also between Newport and Brynmawr via Blaina, were withdrawn on 30th April 1962. Freight closure dates are given in the captions, but it is important to mention here that traffic continued to Ebbw Vale Steelworks until 2001 and that the track was retained in place pending a resumption of passenger services. An hourly frequency to Cardiff was planned for 2007.

PASSENGER SERVICES

The table on the right shows the number of trains arriving in selected years on at least five days in a week.

After the Brynmawr-Nantyglo section was completed in 1906, the GWR ran ten trains over the section, some starting at Newport, while the LNWR operated one or two short journeys. After the 1923 grouping, most GWR trains ran through to the northern limit.

	Nantyglo		Ebbw Vale	
	Weekdays	Sunday	Weekdays	Sunday
1869	5	2	5	2
1889	6	2	6	2
1899	7	2	8	2
1909	14	4	14	4
1929	17	7*	16	8
1949	20	6*	18	6
1962	18	3*	19	1

* To Blaina only

NEWPORT, ABERBEEG, and BRYNMAWR.

July 1929

(Detailed railway timetable for Up and Down services — Week Days and Sundays — for stations including Newport (High St.), Bassaleg Junction, Rogerstone, Risca, Cross Keys, Cwmcarn, Abercarn, Newbridge, Crumlin (L. Level), Llanhilleth, Aberbeeg, Abertillery, Blaina, Nantyglo, Brynmawr; and ABERBEEG and EBBW VALE section with Aberbeeg, Cwm, Victoria, Ebbw Vale.)

E Except Saturdays.   F Fridays and Saturdays.   S Saturdays only.   T Except Saturdays and School Holidays.   W Workmen's Train. 3rd class only.

Mls	Fares.	Dock Street Sta.	mrn	mrn	aft	aft	aft	Suds		Nant-y-glo.		mrn	mrn	aft	aft	aft	Sun'ys
—	0 cl. 2 cl. 3 cl.	Newport ......dep	7	0	1155	3	0	3 57	30	9	0 5 15	fr.Brynmawr	8	25	1115	2	20	4 45	7 25
3	0 8 0 5 0	Bassaleg Junction	7	8	1124	3	11	5 47	43	9	8 5 24	Blaina	8	31	1123	2	28	0 7 3
4	0 10 0 6 0	Tydee	7	13	1129	3	16	5 59	48	9	14 5 29	Abertillery	8	41	1131	2	36	5 10 7 41
6½	1 3 0 9 0	Risca fr.Pontymistr	7	19	1135	3	25	6	57	21	36	Ebbw Vle	8	25	1115	2	20	4 57 25
9	1 8 1 0 0	Cross Keys	7	25	1142	3	31	6	12	8	42	Victoria	3	33	1123	2	28	5 0 7 38
9½	1 11 1 2 0	Chapel Bridge		n	n	n	n		n	n	Cwm	8	38	1128	2	33	5 10 7 38
10½	2 1 1 3 0 10	Abercarn	7	32	1150	3	41	6	29	14	9	35	6 50	Aberbeeg Jnc	8	47	1137	2	45	5 20 7 47
11½	2 4 1 5 0 11	Newbridge	7	37	1155	3	46	6	25	20	9	40	5 56	Crumlin 26.27	9	0	1154	2	55	5 50 8 0
13½	2 6 1 6 1 0	Crumlin 26.27	7	41	12	3	51	6	30	25	9	45	6 0	Newbridge	9	5	1159		8	
15½	3 2 0 1 1 1	Aberbeeg Junction	7	53	1213	4	3	6	40	9	58	6 13	Abercarn	9	10	12	4	3	
18	3 9 2 3 1	19 Cwm	8	2	1224	4	17	6 52		10	7	6 22	Chapel Bridge	n	n	n	n	
19½	4 0 2 6 1 6	19½ Victoria [13]	8	7	12	4	22	6 5		1026	27	Risca 131	9	23	1203	3	8	8 8
21	4 0 2 8 1	21½ Ebbw Vale arr	8	15	1235	4	30	7	5	1020	6 35	Tydee	9	29	1243	3	24	8 29 1148
17	3 6 2 2 1	Abertillery	7	59	1219	4	14	6 49		10	16	19	Bassaleg J.180	9	36	1234	3	31	6 258 36
19½	4 0 2 6 1 6	Blaina {Brynmawr	8	7	1227	4	22	6 57		1026	27	Newprt 28.29	9	45	1245	3	40	6 40 8 45
21	4 0 2 8 1	Nant-y-glo. for	8	15	1235	4	30	7	5	1020	6 35							

June 1869

September 1961

NEWPORT, EBBW VALE, NANTYGLO
and BRYNMAWR
(Second class only)

A About ¼ mile to Bassaleg Station
B About ¼ mile to Crumlin (High Level) Station
E or **E** Except Saturdays
S or **S** Saturdays only

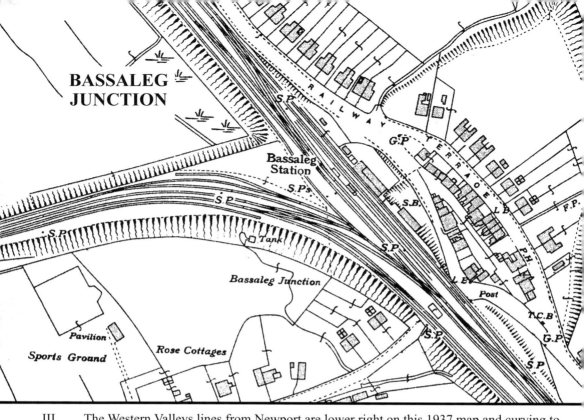

BASSALEG JUNCTION

III.   The Western Valleys lines from Newport are lower right on this 1937 map and curving to the left is the 1865 route of the Brecon & Merthyr Railway. Its Bassaleg station is just off the left border and is illustrated in our *Brecon to Newport* album.

1.   The junction signals are in the background, as a train of mostly empty coal wagons runs north in about 1935. This direction was termed "up", as it was up the valley; on most other lines "up" was the direction to London. As a wartime economy measure, the station was closed from January 1917 to March 1919. (Stations UK)

2.   Signals on the left of this 1956 view (and also to the right of the next one) were for the relief lines, which were in use from 1901 to 1965. There was a fifth line, used as an exchange siding. The station was "Rhymney Junction" from 1850 to 1858. There were four or five men employed here in the 1930s. (Mowat coll./Brunel University)

3.   DMUs were introduced on the Newport-Brynmawr service in 1958 and this example was photographed on 8th August 1959. The stylish "cats whiskers" were replaced with a high visibility panel. The term "Junction" was added in 1924. (S.Rickard/J&J coll.)

4.   The massive signal box once had 95 levers and is seen from a railtour on the down relief line in 1965. The platform lines were taken out of use in 1963 and the box followed on 9th December 1968. (P.J.Garland/R.S.Carpenter coll.)

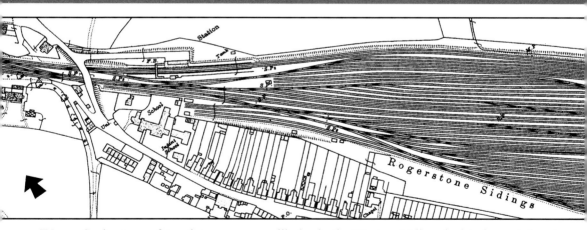

IV.   Coal wagons from the numerous collieries in the Western Valleys had to be sorted and made up into trains for various English destinations and the Welsh docks. Thus a marshalling yard was developed south of the station from 1885 onwards. There were four running lines flanked by about ten sidings each side, the western group being used by returning empties. Further expansion came in 1900, when passenger lines were added on the east side of the complex and three signal boxes were provided. A hump was added at the north end in 1931, by which time there were eight running lines and over 30 sidings. The peak capacity was 280 wagons per hour. The 1920 map at 15ins to 1 mile shows that Castle Steel Works was connected to the yard and also to the Brecon to Newport line, which is lower right. Near the schools on the left, there was a signal box until 5th November 1978; it was known as Middle Box and had 47 levers.

SOUTH OF ROGERSTONE

5.   A northward view from the same train features the quadruple track, which was completed almost to Risca (Pontymister South) in 1901. Rogerstone South box had 87 levers and was closed on 9th December 1968. The down marshalling yard is beyond it, this closing on the same day. Back in 1885, a line was laid (on the left) to Nettlefold's steelworks, later GK&N Ltd, Castle Works. It was used by Northern Aluminium from 1947. (P.J.Garland/R.S.Carpenter coll.)

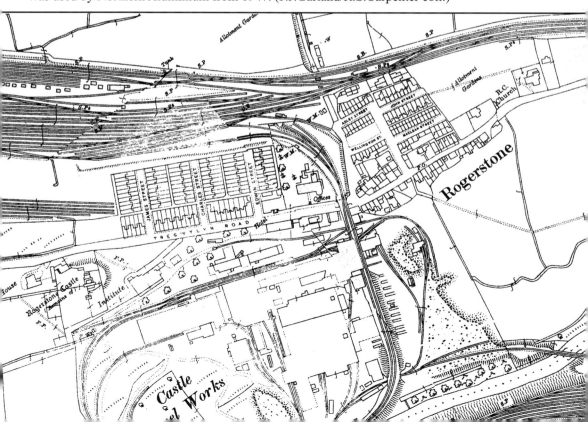

ROGERSTONE

6.　　A small station called Tydu was opened here in August 1851 and renamed Rogerstone on 20th October 1898. This postcard depicts the new station provided on the realigned passenger lines to the east of the marshalling yards where traffic ceased on 28th November 1966. A staff of four was reduced to two in the late 1920s. (Lens of Sutton coll.)

7.　　A view southeast from the A467 in 1958 includes an 0-6-0PT standing on the hump at the north end of the marshalling yard, part of which is visible on the right. Featured is the Hump Control cabin, which was built on top of the existing upside waiting room. (Stations UK)

8.   From the same viewpoint as the previous photograph, we see the main building again. The new track alignment was brought into use in November 1981, this facilitating major road works. Seen on 22nd October 1982 is no. 37291 with a Llanwern to Waunllwyd working. The redundant station building has since been demolished. (D.H.Mitchell)

NORTH OF ROGERSTONE

9.   Rogerstone North box was over ½ mile north of the station and opened on 1st February 1931. It had 43 levers and controlled a multitude of crossovers, as well as the power station sidings, seen on the right in this 1965 southward view. The box closed on 15th November 1970, the eastern part of the yard having been abandoned in 1968. The remainder lasted until 1977. Loaded trains had entered the hump approach lines here. The relief lines lasted until 1970, by then giving access to the Sirhowy Valley only. (P.J.Garland/R.S.Carpenter coll.)

TYNYCWM HALT

10.   The island platform opened on 17th April 1935 and was in use until the end of passenger service. South of the halt, there was Tynycwm signal box (29 levers), also Rogerstone Brick & Stone siding, between about 1907 and 1926. This southward view is from June 1962 and the relief lines are on the right. (M.Hale)

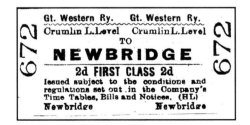

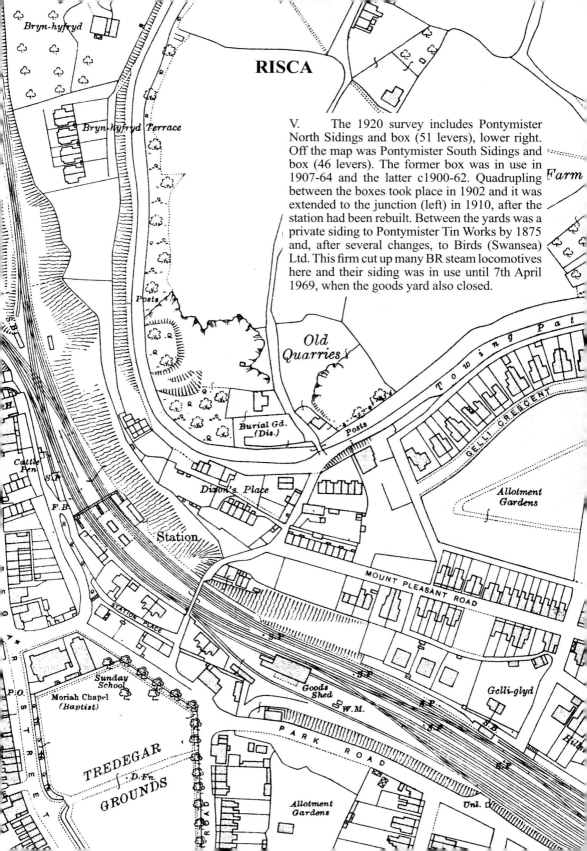

RISCA

V. The 1920 survey includes Pontymister North Sidings and box (51 levers), lower right. Off the map was Pontymister South Sidings and box (46 levers). The former box was in use in 1907-64 and the latter c1900-62. Quadrupling between the boxes took place in 1902 and it was extended to the junction (left) in 1910, after the station had been rebuilt. Between the yards was a private siding to Pontymister Tin Works by 1875 and, after several changes, to Birds (Swansea) Ltd. This firm cut up many BR steam locomotives here and their siding was in use until 7th April 1969, when the goods yard also closed.

11.   This southward panorama predates the 1910 rebuilding, as only two platforms are present. The train is in LNWR livery and thus bound for the Sirhowy Valley. (Lens of Sutton coll.)

12.   A badly printed postcard shows the junction before alteration in 1910. The signal box was completed in 1886. Our route to Aberbeeg is on the right. (D.Edge coll.)

13.　　The same viewpoint 50 or so years later features an 0-6-0PT signalled for Sirhowy and a DMU leaving for Ebbw Vale. The 57-lever signal box was in use until 22nd December 1968, when all the points were taken out of use. The lines to the left were not used after 4th May 1970. (D.Edge coll.)

14.　　This is the view from a DMU from Brynmawr, not long before withdrawal of passenger service in April 1962. There had been a staff of 70 here in 1923, reducing to 50 ten years later. (D.Edge coll.)

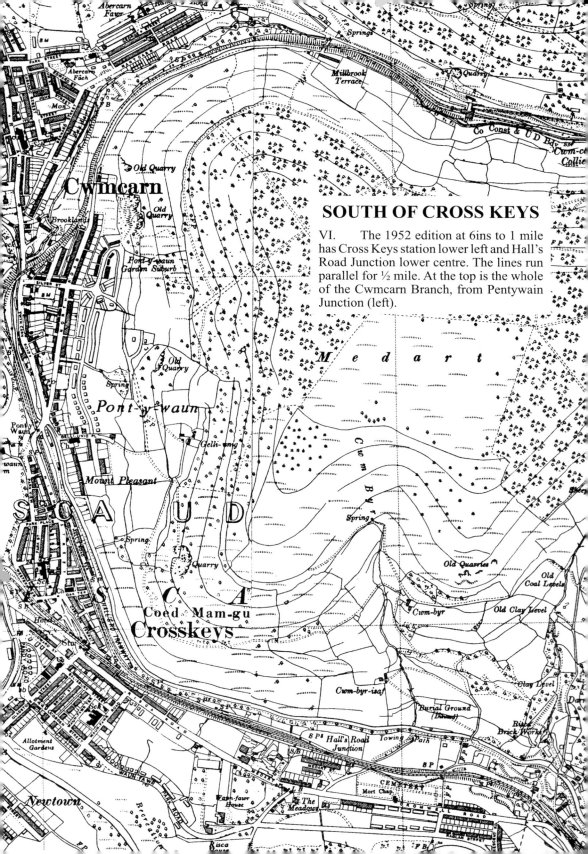

SOUTH OF CROSS KEYS

VI.   The 1952 edition at 6ins to 1 mile has Cross Keys station lower left and Hall's Road Junction lower centre. The lines run parallel for ½ mile. At the top is the whole of the Cwmcarn Branch, from Pentywain Junction (left).

15.	Lime Kiln Junction was the point at which traffic for Hall's Road left the main line after 21st December 1967, when the junction further north closed. This box had 29 levers and operated lifting barriers from March 1980. No. 25115 is northbound with the weed killing train on 9th May 1979. (M.J.Hughes)

16.	The branch to Cwmcarn Colliery ran east from the Hall's Road line at Pontywain Junction. The end of the branch is seen on 22nd March 1962. (C.H.A.Townley/J.A.Peden coll.)

17.	No. 37185 heads south on 22nd October 1982, having just passed the site of Cross Keys station. On the left is Hall's Road, which then carried the output of Oakdale Colliery. (D.H.Mitchell)

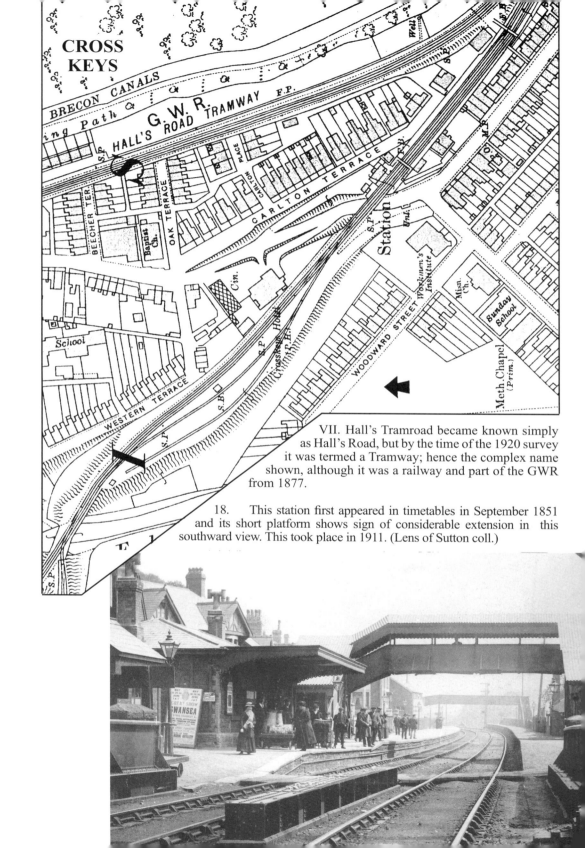

CROSS KEYS

BRECON CANALS

ng Path

HALL'S ROAD TRAMWAY F.P.

G.W.R.

BEECHER TER.

Baptist Ch.

OAK TERRACE

CARLTON PLACE

CARLTON TERRACE

Ctn.

School

WESTERN TERRACE

S.P.

S.P.

Crosskeys Hotel

Station

Woodward Street Workmen's Institute

WOODWARD STREET

Misn. Ch.

Sunday School

Meth. Chapel (Prim.)

VII. Hall's Tramroad became known simply as Hall's Road, but by the time of the 1920 survey it was termed a Tramway; hence the complex name shown, although it was a railway and part of the GWR from 1877.

18. This station first appeared in timetables in September 1851 and its short platform shows sign of considerable extension in this southward view. This took place in 1911. (Lens of Sutton coll.)

19.   Looking in the other direction, we see the 25-lever box, which was in use in 1901-58. There was a staff of 12 in 1923, but this was halved by 1934.
(Lens of Sutton coll.)

20.   A southward panorama on 21st January 1958 shows the extent of the goods yard, which was in use from about 1901 to 23rd March 1964. Hall's Road and the canal are on the hillside on the left.
(S.C.L.Phillips/
D.K.Jones coll.)

21. The public footbridge in the distance had only one flight of steps, as its left end was almost level with Hall's Road. This is the neglected scene in about 1970. (Lens of Sutton coll.)

22. This picture was taken from the footbridge in the background of photograph 21. No. 37185 is passing the site of the station with a load of coal on 22nd October 1982. The background is as in picture 19. (D.H.Mitchell)

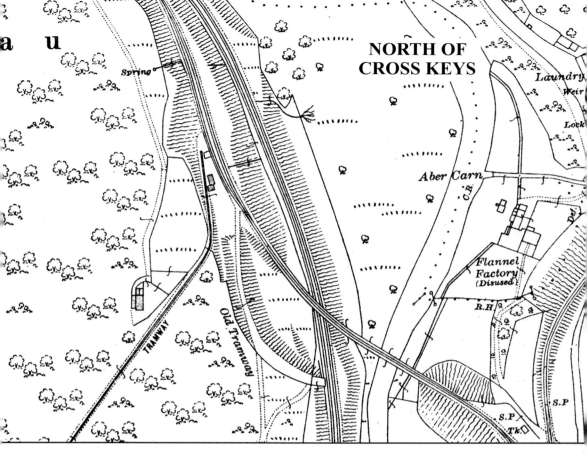

Spring

Aber Carn

Laundry

Weir

Lock

Flannel Factory (Disused)

R.H

S.P

S.P

Tk

TRAMWAY

Old Tramway

VIII.   This 1920 extract helps to explain the next photograph. On the right is Hall's Road, just north of Pentywain Junction, the curve on the extreme right being the first part of its Cwmcarn Branch. The double track is our route, which passes under Hall's Road. The tramway on the left was from Pont Hall Quarry; the loop siding on Hall's Road was in use from about 1909 until 1936.

23.   This eastward panorama has the single line of Hall's Road on clean ballast, as it has been realigned to eliminate the sharp bends at each end of the abandoned viaduct on the right. The western bend is marked on the map as "Old Tramway". North of here was Chapel Bridge station, until 1876. The Hall's Road Tramway was subject to a 999 year lease and this has recently created legal problems, following closure and partial lifting of the track. (M.Dart coll.)

CWMCARN

24. The station was opened on 2nd March 1925 and was close to the site of the earlier Chapel Bridge station. This is a southward view from a DMU. There was a Pagoda shelter on the opposite platform.
(D.Edge coll.)

IX. The 1920 survey shows Chapel Bridge itself, but neither station existed at that time.

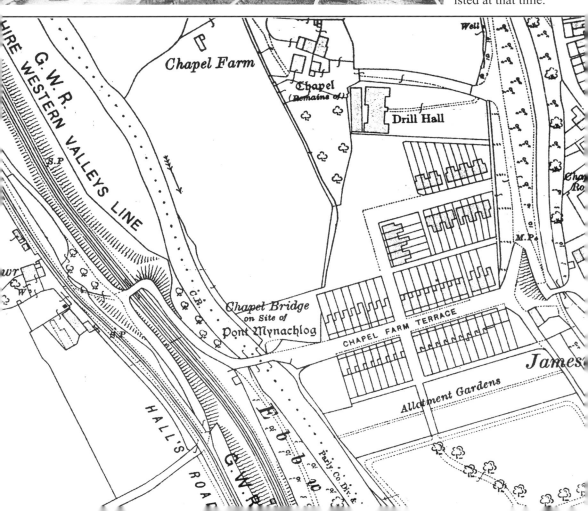

SOUTH OF ABERCARN

X. The line branching right at the centre of this 6ins to 1 mile map of 1922 ran to the Prince of Wales Colliery until 29th August 1963. The signal box is in the fork; it closed that day and had a 27-lever frame. Three tracks ran north; the right one was the 1899 down loop and at the north end of it was Abercarn Loop box (20 levers), which also closed on the same day. The station is on this and the next map.

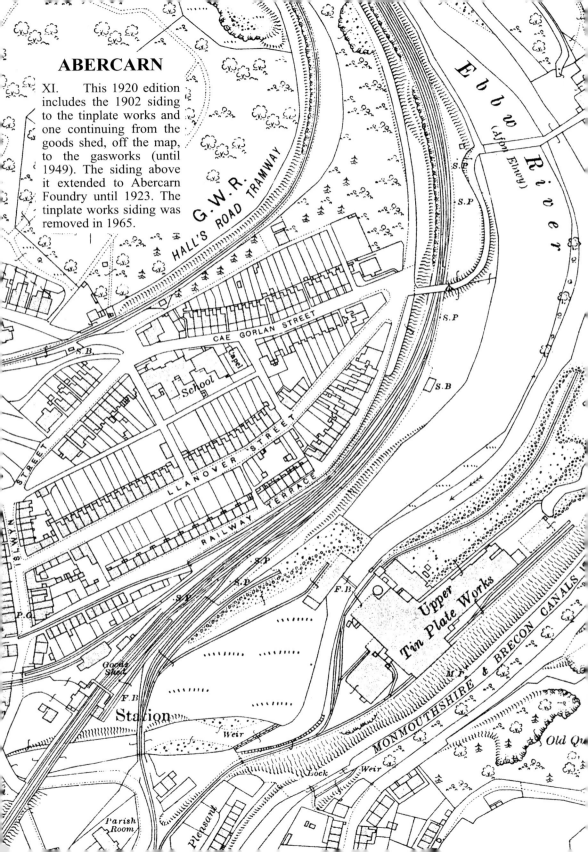

ABERCARN

XI. This 1920 edition includes the 1902 siding to the tinplate works and one continuing from the goods shed, off the map, to the gasworks (until 1949). The siding above it extended to Abercarn Foundry until 1923. The tinplate works siding was removed in 1965.

25.   This was another of the original stations, but the footbridge was a late addition. This is a southward view from 1958. (Stations UK)

26.   There had been about 25 employees here in the 1930s. We look north after closure to passengers; the goods yard had been on the left, but this closed earlier, on 7th December 1959. The signal box is in the distance; it had 35 levers and lasted from 1905 to 1968. (D.Edge coll.)

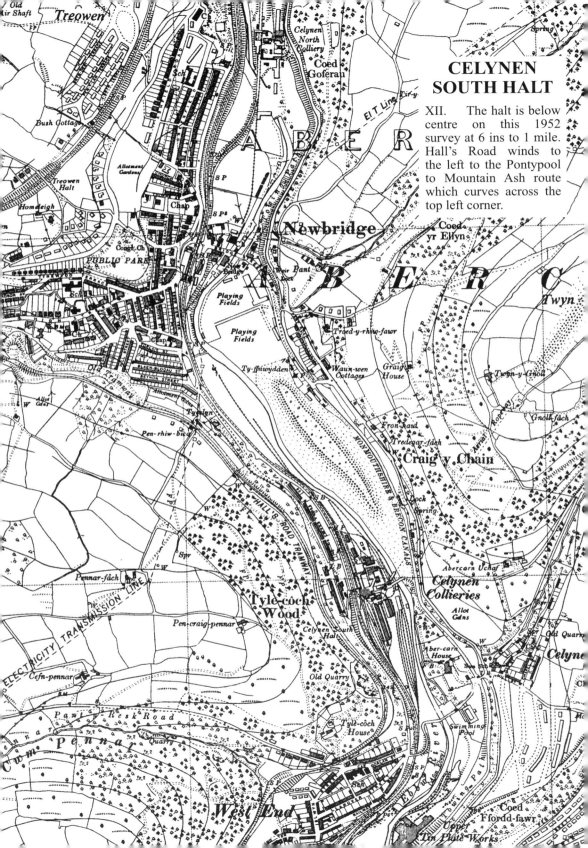

CELYNEN
SOUTH HALT

XII.   The halt is below centre on this 1952 survey at 6 ins to 1 mile. Hall's Road winds to the left to the Pontypool to Mountain Ash route which curves across the top left corner.

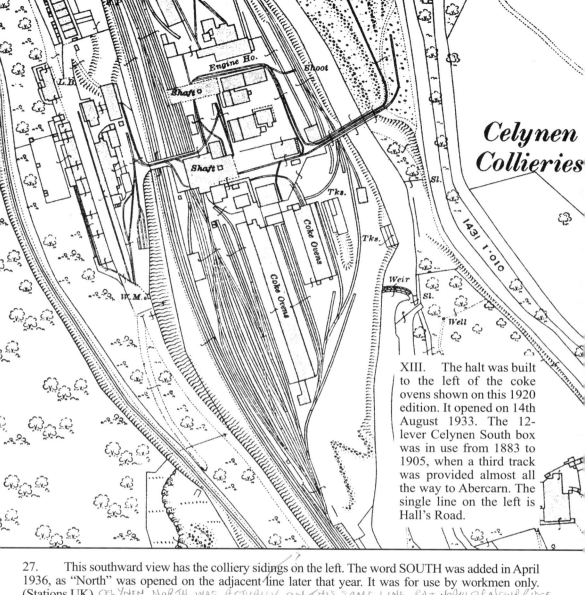

Celynen Collieries

XIII.   The halt was built to the left of the coke ovens shown on this 1920 edition. It opened on 14th August 1933. The 12-lever Celynen South box was in use from 1883 to 1905, when a third track was provided almost all the way to Abercarn. The single line on the left is Hall's Road.

27.   This southward view has the colliery sidings on the left. The word SOUTH was added in April 1936, as "North" was opened on the adjacent line later that year. It was for use by workmen only. (Stations UK) CELYNEN NORTH WAS ACTUALLY ON THIS SAME LINE BUT NORTH OF NEWBRIDGE SEE 34

28.   Working at the colliery on 14th June 1965 was *Menelaus*, Peckett no. 1889 of 1935. (Rev. A.Newman/ C.G.Maggs coll.)

29.   National Coal Board and BR tracks were in great contrast when the NCB's shunter was photographed on 24th September 1984, preparing a train for departure. These sidings were added in 1926. There was a small signal box at the north end of the site from 1891 to 1968. (D.H.Mitchell)

30.   Minutes later, no. 37164 arrived, having used a crossover, out of view, between the two pictures. It will run south and then reverse onto its train, which was destined for Llanwern Steelworks. (D.H.Mitchell)

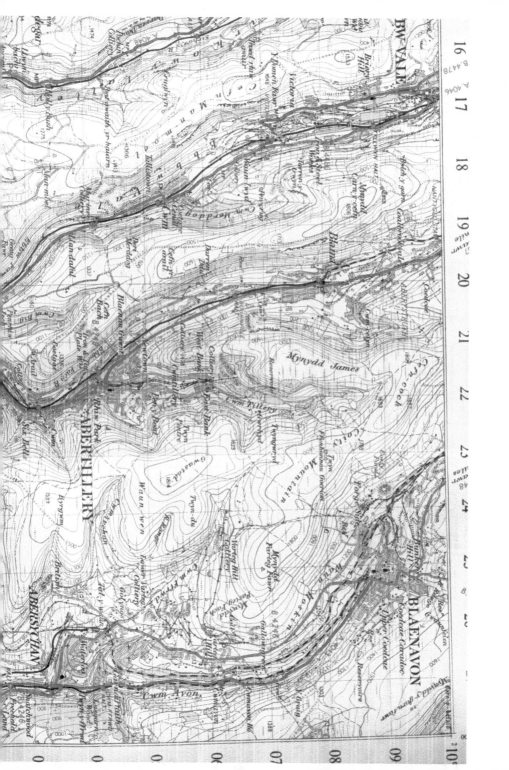

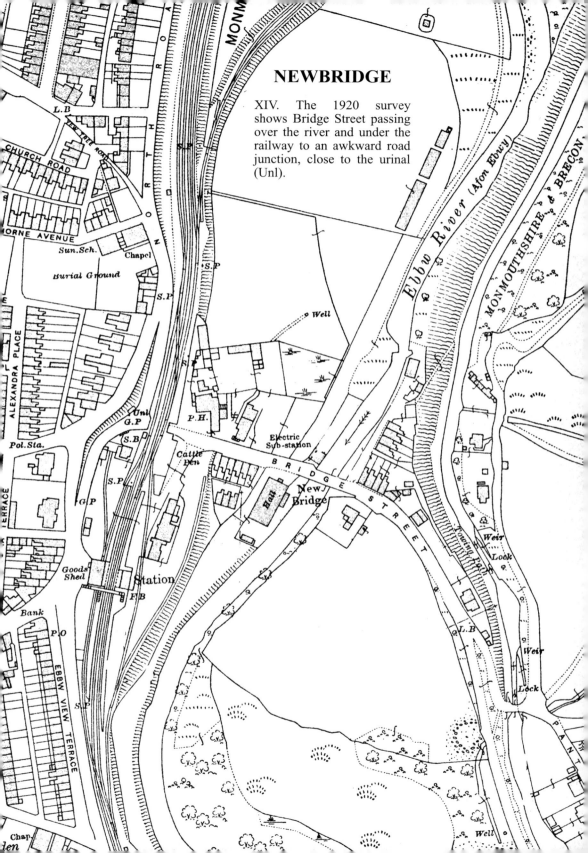

NEWBRIDGE

XIV. The 1920 survey shows Bridge Street passing over the river and under the railway to an awkward road junction, close to the urinal (Unl).

31. A ~~north~~ _South_ ward panorama from the footbridge includes both goods loops. The small signal box was replaced in 1887 and distant signal arms became yellow instead of red, as here. (Lens of Sutton coll.)

32. The manning level was around 14 in the 1930s. This postcard was produced before the GWR introduced cast iron seat ends and removed interesting chimneys. The left bridge span is over the goods yard loop. (Lens of Sutton coll.)

33.   The signal box had a 33-lever frame and lasted in use until 16th October 1968. Beyond it is Celynen North Colliery. The goods yard was still in use; it closed on 7th April 1969. (Lens of Sutton coll.)

CELYNEN NORTH HALT

34.   The halt was opened on 10th August 1936 and was within sight of Crumlin Viaduct. They were photographed on 14th July 1958. The halt was intended for miners and did not appear in public timetables. (R.M.Casserley)

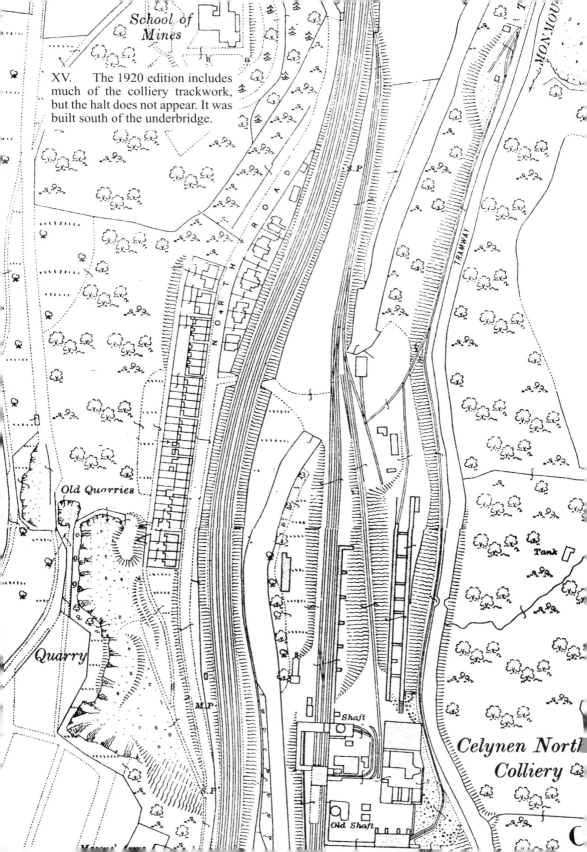

School of
Mines

XV.   The 1920 edition includes
much of the colliery trackwork,
but the halt does not appear. It was
built south of the underbridge.

S.P

NORTH ROAD

TRAMWAY

Old Quarries

Tank

Quarry

M.P.

Shaft

S.P.

Celynen North
Colliery

Old Shaft

35. Pit props were being unloaded on 14th June 1965 when the NCB's Hawthorn Leslie no. 3923 of 1937 was photographed. Crumlin Viaduct is in the distance.
(Rev. A.Newman/ C.G.Maggs)

36. A coal train is northbound in about 1970 as we examine passenger access. This was via a long subway from the hoarding on the right and then over the footbridge. However, colliery workers did not have to pass under the tracks.
(Lens of Sutton coll.)

37. No. 6976 is running from the south on 21st May 1973 with empties for a colliery further north. Traffic here ceased on 31st December 1979.
(T.Heavyside)

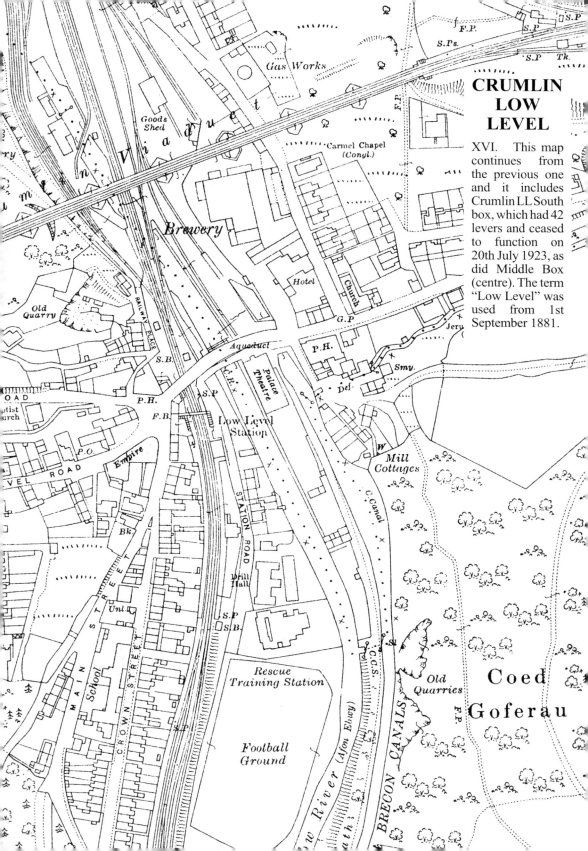

CRUMLIN LOW LEVEL

XVI. This map continues from the previous one and it includes Crumlin LL South box, which had 42 levers and ceased to function on 20th July 1923, as did Middle Box (centre). The term "Low Level" was used from 1st September 1881.

Gas Works

Goods Shed

Carmel Chapel (Cong¹.)

Brewery

Old Quarry

Hotel

Church

G.P

Jeru

Aquaduct

P.H.

S.B.

Smy.

Def.

P.H.

Palace Theatre

S.P.

F.B.

Low Level Station

P.O.

Empire

W

Mill Cottages

Bk.

ROAD

C. Canal

Unl.

Drill Hall

S.P.
S.B.

C.C.S.

Rescue Training Station

Old Quarries

C o e d

River (Afon Ebwy)

BRECON CANALS

Football Ground

G o f e r a u

38.   Featured here is Middle Box (19 levers), also known as Crossing Box. The level crossing was replaced in 1923 by the bridge shown on the map. There were 16 men employed here at that time. (G.M.Perkins/R.S.Carpenter coll.)

39.   The 1923 bridge span is evident, as is the small aqueduct (lower left), mentioned on the map. In the distance is Celynen North Colliery and the 1923 signal box is on the down platform. (G.Davis/B.King coll.)

40.   The station is in the distance as 0-6-2T no. 6656 runs north with a SLS Special on 6th May 1962. The lines on the right served Crumlin Navigation Colliery until 22nd January 1969. On the left is the goods yard, which was in use until 7th November 1966. The goods shed dated from 1910. (D.Edge coll.)

41.   A DMU stands near the 1923 box, not long before closure to passengers in 1962. Crumlin Viaduct is featured in our *Pontypool to Mountain Ash* album and was dismantled carefully from a temporary Bailey bridge above it in 1965. (D.Lawrence)

42.	The station house and the base of the signal box are on the left as no. 6985 passes through the remains on 21st May 1973. However, much of the building complex of the colliery survives. (T.Heavyside)

NORTH OF CRUMLIN

43.	This is the opposite view to picture no. 40 and was taken from the 1857 Crumlin Viaduct on 11th April 1955. Crumlin Navigation Colliery opened in 1908. (H.C.Casserley)

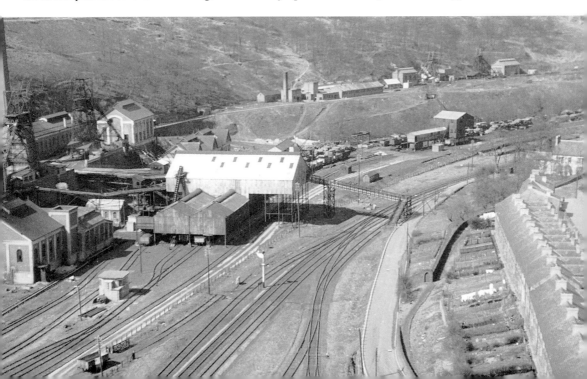

SOUTH OF
LLANHILLETH

XVII.   The station is on the left page of this 1920 survey and above the goods shed on the right page is North box. The colliery lines are lower right.

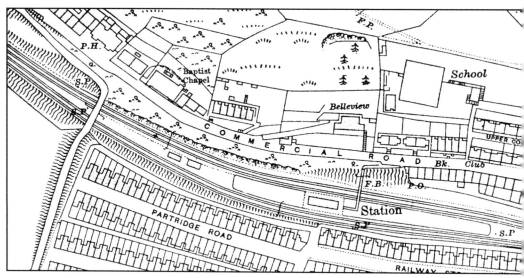

44.   Llanhilleth Colliery (left) was recorded from the hillside on 9th July 1953, along with Llanhilleth Middle box (97 levers), in use until 17th May 1964. Behind the camera was South box, which had 41 levers and closed on 11th December 1967. It was replaced by Llanhilleth Colliery Outlet ground frame until closure of the sidings on 9th June 1970. (D.Edge coll.)

45.   A closer view of Llanhilleth Steam Coal Colliery in August 1960 shows that many alterations to the structures had taken place. From left to right are two sidings, four running lines and (beyond the signal) two tracks that merge into one to form the 1855 connection to the High Level lines. This link only ever carried workmen and freight. The loco is shunting stock into the coal screens siding. (P.Chancellor coll.)

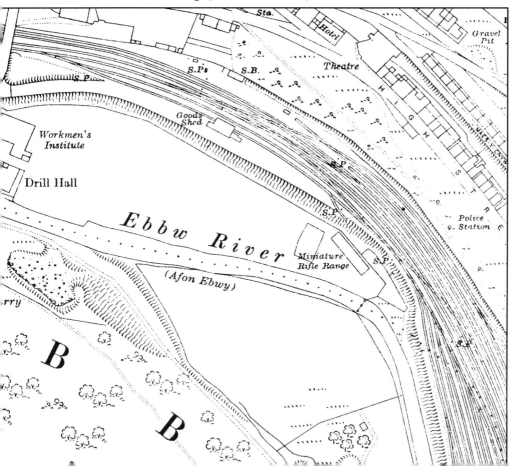

LLANHILLETH

46.   Passengers were conveyed from August 1853, according to timetable records. This eastward postcard view was intended to show the hillside town. There were around 26 employees here in the late 1920s. (D.Edge coll.)

47.   Looking in the same direction in September 1960, we see 2-8-0T no. 5241 and North Box. It had 51 levers in its frame and functioned until 17th May 1964. (D.K.Jones coll.)

48. The somersault signals are evident as 0-6-2T no. 6693 blows off on 14th October 1961. The train is the 12.35pm (Saturdays only) from Brynmawr to Newport. Note the inclined path to the station. (R.E.Toop)

49. The lower part of the town is included in this 1962 panorama. Freight service was withdrawn on the same day as passenger service. (Stations UK)

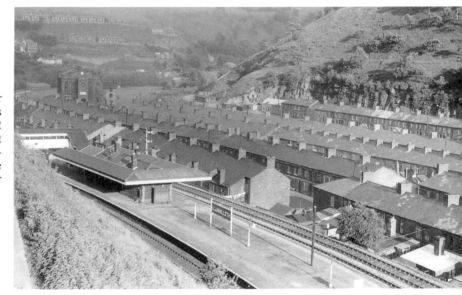

50. Nos 37901 and 37903 have just passed the site of the station on 8th September 1998, while hauling a load of steel from Margam to Ebbw Vale, for conversion to tinplate. (D.H.Mitchell)

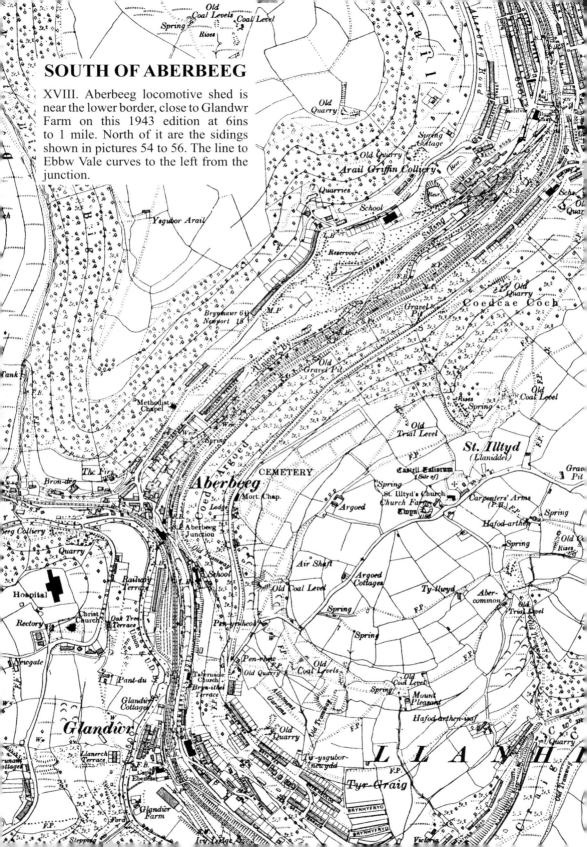

SOUTH OF ABERBEEG

XVIII. Aberbeeg locomotive shed is near the lower border, close to Glandwr Farm on this 1943 edition at 6ins to 1 mile. North of it are the sidings shown in pictures 54 to 56. The line to Ebbw Vale curves to the left from the junction.

51. The new locomotive depot was photographed soon after completion in 1919. The coal stage is under the water tank, a standard GWR design. The shed code was ABG, becoming 86H in 1948.
(GWR Magazine)

52. Three of the four running lines are visible, along with the single line depot connection. The chimney on the right was for the sand dryer. This panorama is from 1939. There were 37 locomotives allocated here in 1947, all tank engines.
(R.S.Carpenter coll.)

53. The wagon on the left is at the end of the coal stage siding, on 25th September 1956. The shed was in use until December 1964. Access to the depot was controlled by the 33-lever Aberbeeg South box, this closing on 30th July 1964. The main shed building was still in use in 2006 as part of a foundry.
(S.Rickard/
B.J.Miller coll.)

54.   These sidings were situated between the engine shed and the station; they are seen in December 1956 as two trains pass on the main lines. The relief lines are the outer ones on each side of the trains. (P.Q.Treloar)

55.   Two different trains occupy the relief lines on the same December day; two class 9F 2-10-0s work hard against the gradient with a train of imported iron ore from Newport Docks to Ebbw Vale Steelworks. (P.Q.Treloar)

56.   Half the yard was taken out of use in 1976 and the remainder in 1978. No. 37301 was recorded on 26th September 1980, along with Aberbeeg Junction box, which had 65 levers. (D.H.Mitchell)

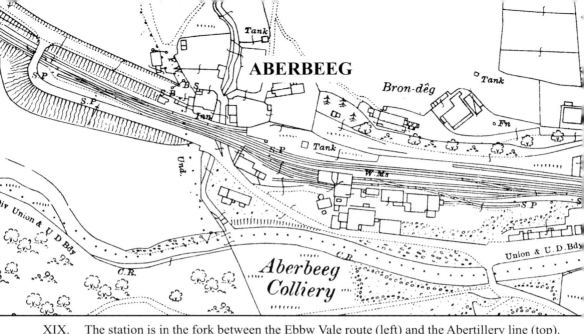

XIX.   The station is in the fork between the Ebbw Vale route (left) and the Abertillery line (top). The shed near the bottom of the right page housed locomotives until 1919.

57.   The route from Llanhilleth (lower) was quadruple from 12th April 1903. The junction is seen in about 1935, when there was a staff of 61 on the payroll of this station. (Stations UK)

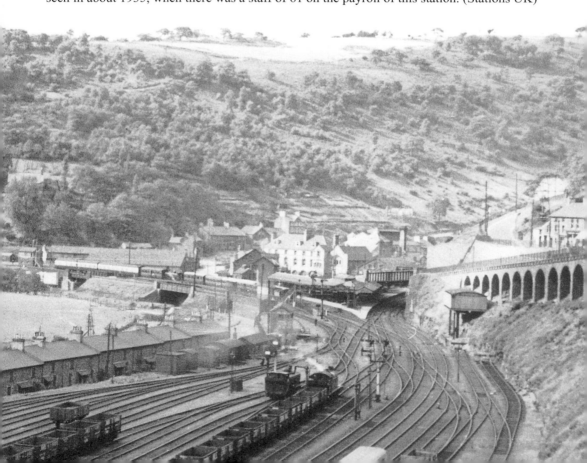

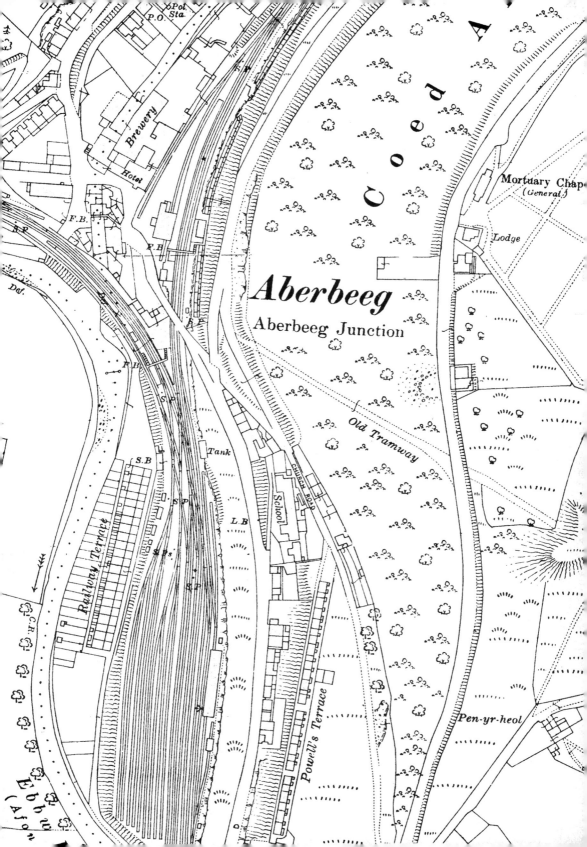

Coed A

Aberbeeg

Aberbeeg Junction

Old Tramway

Mortuary Chap
(General)

Lodge

Pen-yr-heol

Brewery

Hotel

P.O. Sta.
Pol.

F.B.

F.B.

F.B.

F.B.

S.P.

S.P.

S.P.

S.P.

S.P.

S.P.

S.P.

S.B.

Tank

L.B.

School

Church Road

Railway Terrace

Powell's Terrace

C.R.

Def.

Ebbw
(Afon)

58.   Aberbeeg shed housed more 0-6-0PTs of this type than any other class. This one is passing through the Brynmawr platform with wagons with extended sides for the conveyance of coke. It is December 1956. (P.Q.Treloar)

59.   We move to 1st September 1957 and witness 2-6-2T no. 4237 on the line from Ebbw Vale, which is here parallel to the Ebbw River. Aberbeeg Colliery is in the left background. (M.Dart)

60.   A DMU from Ebbw Vale waits to depart south in about 1960. The station was gas lit to the end. (J.Parker/ H.Davies coll.)

61.   A closer look at the Ebbw Vale up platform in 1962 reveals that there is a starting signal on the opposite platform, for trains reversing here. The goods loop is included in this view. (P.J.Garland/ R.S.Carpenter coll.)

62.   The date is 6th May 1962 and passenger service has just been withdrawn. Heading the SLS Special is 0-6-2T no. 6656. (D.Edge coll.)

63.   A view in the same direction as picture 57 reveals a changing scene. The former no. 55016 is in departmental service on 22nd October 1982. The route had been singled in July 1981; the signal box lasted in use until 14th December 1997. It was still standing, although derelict in 2006. (D.H.Mitchell)

64.   No. 37164 is seen on 24th September 1985 with the 10.05 Rose Heyworth Colliery to Llanwern Steelworks working. The former is three miles to the north of Aberbeeg. (D.H.Mitchell)

SIX BELLS HALT

XX. Known as Arail Griffin Colliery initially, Six Bells Colliery sidings were in use until 30th November 1980. The halt opened on 27th September 1937 and was just beyond the northern border of this 1920 map.

Workmen's Institute

P. H.

CHAPEL ROAD

Baptist Chapel

W. M.

S. P.

S. P.

C. R.

SIX BELLS ROAD

Spring Cottage

Reservoir

iery

Reservoir

Shaft

Shaft

F. B.

Def.

S. P.

S. P.

VICTORIA ROAD

Sch

il Griffin Siding

W. M.

W. M.

S. P.

M. P.

Old Quarry

65. This view is from the colliery eastwards to Victoria Road before the up loop came into use in May 1914. The track beyond the train is the 1902 down loop. (D.Edge coll.)

66. The four tracks reduced to two south of the halt. A loop north thereof served two small collieries. No. 4252 was photographed on this loop, which was in use until June 1964. (D.K.Jones coll.)

67. A view south in 1962 includes the footbridge to the platform. The train obscures the private siding for J.Lancaster & Co. Ltd.; this was in use in 1891-1980. North of the halt was the 35-lever Cwmnantygroes box, which closed on 11th October 1964. (Stations UK)

68.   Six Bells Colliery sidings are largely obscured by the foliage in this May 1973 panorama. The down goods loop went in 1964 and the up one followed in 1970. (T.Heavyside)

69.   No. 25318 waits with the weed killing train at Six Bells Colliery siding on 8th May 1979, which was not used after 5th January 1981. (M.J.Hughes)

← —————— XXI. The 1920 survey shows the position of the station since 1893. It had been nearer the junction of the Cwmtillery Branch, which ran for one mile northwards (top). The tinplate works was in production from 1846 to 1957, but Tin Works Junction box lasted until 11th October 1964. It had 20 levers and was just beyond the lower border of the map. The premises were used for wagon repairs in their final years.

70.   This view southeast is from about 1905; the route northwards from the junction had been doubled in 1884. There were 59 employees here in 1929 and still 48 in 1938. (Lens of Sutton coll.)

71.   A postcard from the same era reveals that the platform was of timber construction to reduce weight on the made-up land on the side of the valley. (Lens of Sutton coll.)

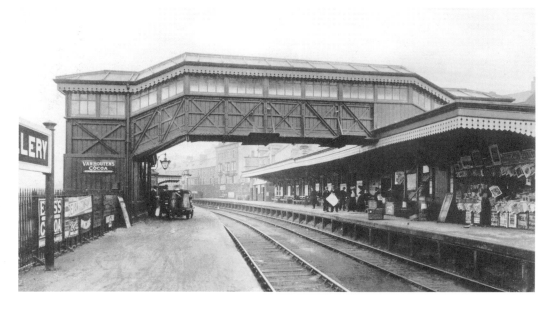

72. A photograph from about 1935 includes the iron-clad parcels room and the lamp room, always spaced from other buildings for safety reasons.
(Stations UK)

73. A post-passenger closure northward view includes the water tank, not seen in other pictures. This part of the route was singled on 3rd May 1971.
(Lens of Sutton coll.)

74. No. 37294 works a ballast train on 29th April 1979 and passes Abertillery gasworks. This was not rail connected; presumably there was enough coal available locally.
(M.J.Hughes)

CWMTILLERY BRANCH

XXII. The full length of the branch is shown on the right of the 1943 edition at 6 ins to 1 mile. Rose Heyworth Colliery is top left, on the line to Brynmawr.

75. This postcard view is southwards near the bottom of map XXII and features Foundry Bridge and beyond it are the sidings at the top of map XXI. In the foreground are the sidings leading to Gray Pit. The line up the valley was doubled in 1899. (D. Edge coll.)

XXIII. The map continues from the top of no. XXI, the boundary being at Foundry Bridge. The branch opened in 1858 and closed in 1961. It had a ruling gradient of 1 in 24 and thus never carried passengers.

NORTH OF ABERTILLERY

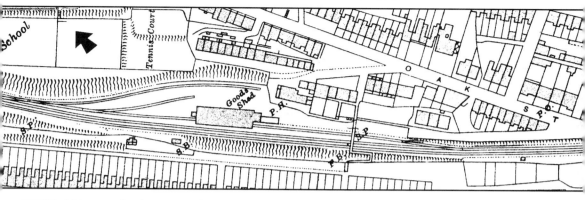

XXIV. This map is almost continuous with no. XXI; Oak Street has been seen on the left of pictures 70 and 72. There was a six-ton crane listed here in 1938. The goods yard was in use from 1895 until 1969, although only used for coal after 1966.

76. No. 6997 is shunting at the new mine at Rose Heyworth on 21st May 1973. This mine was developed in 1956-59 by creating a 1200yd long drift at a 1 in 5 gradient and linking it with the Cwmtillery complex. (T.Heavyside)

77. A close look at the new premises on 8th May 1979 includes no. 25318. The line northwards was closed in 1976 and traffic southward ceased in 1984. Rose Heyworth North box (16 levers) closed in 1953, South box (27 levers) in 1960 and their replacement (47 levers) in 1964. (M.J.Hughes)

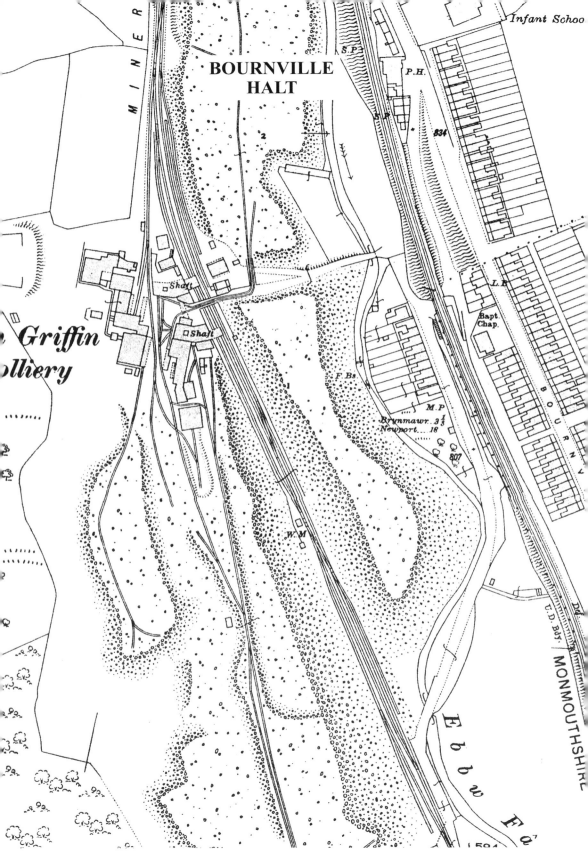

BOURNVILLE
HALT

Infant Schoo

S.P.

P.H.

S.P.

834

Shaft

L.B.

Griffin

Bapt.
Chap.

olliery

F.Bs.

M.P.

Brynmawr 3¾
Newport 18

807

W.M.

U. D. Bdy

MONMOUTHSHIRE

Ebbw Fa

MINER

← ———— XXV. The halt is not annotated on this 1920 map, as it did not open to the public until 30th October 1933. However, careful examination will reveal that it is drawn on it near the Baptist Chapel, as it was being used by miners by 3rd June 1915. South Griffin Colliery sidings (left) were in use between about 1885 and 1937, but the northern part was retained for an electrical sub-station until 1952.

78.   Looking south in July 1957, we see the backs of the houses in Bournville Road. This stop was around 1½ miles north of Abertillery. The original name was Tylers Arms Platform. (R.M.Casserley)

79.   The disused structure was recorded in about 1970. The halt was about one mile south of Blaina, but we are looking in the opposite direction. The track was doubled in this vicinity in 1880, singled in 1964 and closed in 1976. (Lens of Sutton coll.)

BLAINA

XXVI. The 1922 edition at 6ins to 1 mile has Blaina station near the bottom and Nantyglo's top left.

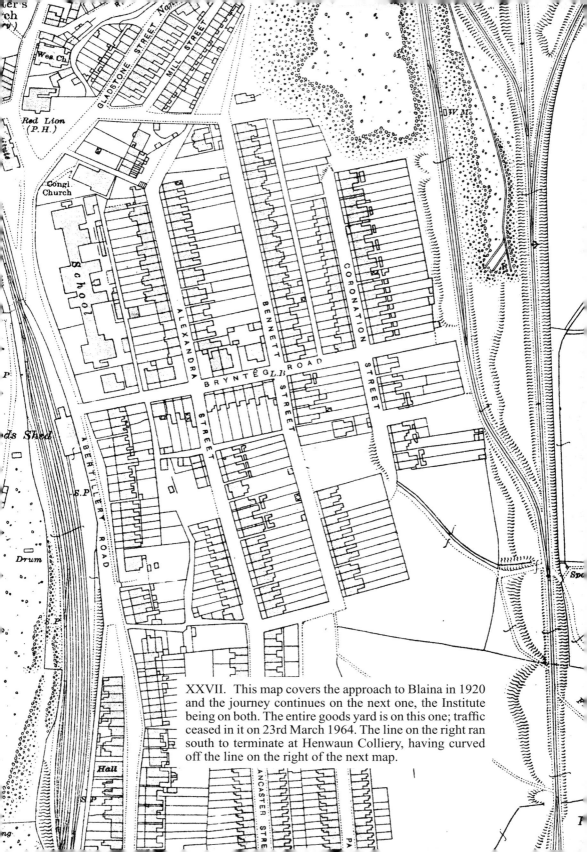

XXVII. This map covers the approach to Blaina in 1920 and the journey continues on the next one, the Institute being on both. The entire goods yard is on this one; traffic ceased in it on 23rd March 1964. The line on the right ran south to terminate at Henwaun Colliery, having curved off the line on the right of the next map.

XXVIII. The line to Nantyglo is top left, it being single from
half way up the page. The works area originally produced
iron. The line on the right also served Lower Deep Pit.

80.   The staffing level was around 15 in the 1930s, but this photograph is from about 1914 and includes a train bound for Newport. (Lens of Sutton coll.)

81.   The gasworks was photographed in about 1951, but it had lost its siding in 1944. This was in use between 1911 and 1937, although it does not show on the map. The Brynmawr & Blaina Gas Company consumed about 4000 tons of coal per annum between those dates, after which time coke oven gas was obtained from Blaenavon. (Wales Gas Board)

82.　　The footbridge roof had long gone when these two photographs were taken in the mid-1960s. The Pagoda shelter is on the up platform. (Lens of Sutton coll.)

83.　　The southward [NORTH] view features the 42-lever signal box, which closed on 11th October 1964. Work is in progress on the right rodding tunnel. (Lens of Sutton coll.)

⟶ XXIX. This map continues from the top of the previous one and has our route north on the left. North Blaina Colliery is on the right. The lines top left converge at Coalbrookvale, where there was a 37-lever signal box until 1st November 1953.

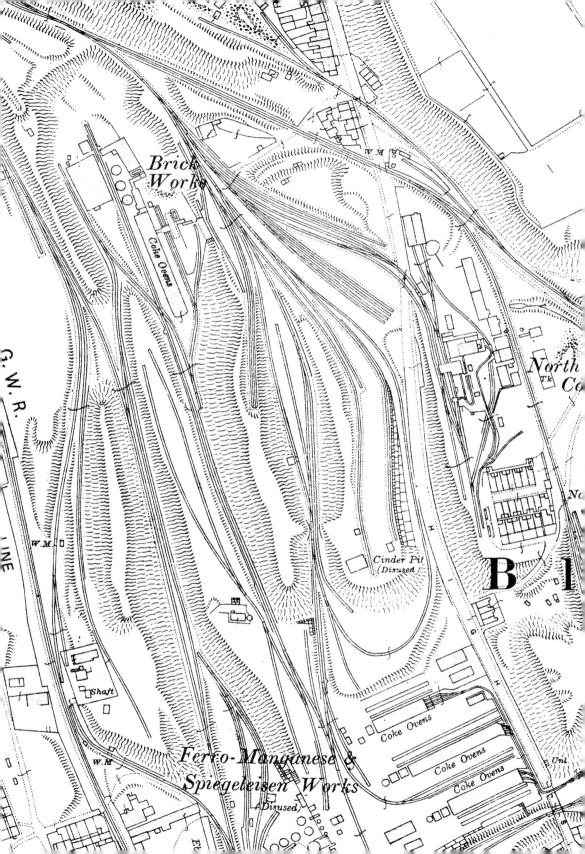

Brick Works

Coke Ovens

G.W.R.

LINE

W.M.

Shaft

W.M.

W.M.

Ferro-Manganese &
Spiegeleisen Works
(Disused)

W.M.

Cinder Pit
(Disused)

North Co

Tk

B

Coke Ovens

Coke Ovens

Coke Ovens

84.   The Welsh Railway Society Special on 5th October 1968 reached the junction of the line to North Blaina Colliery, which is in the centre of map XXVI. The line north of the junction to Brynmawr was used by through freight trains until 4th November 1963. (D.Edge coll.)

NANTYGLO

XXX.   The survey of 1920 includes a private siding, which was used intermittently between 1907 and 1949, also earlier in around 1875. We have now climbed to over 1000ft above sea level.

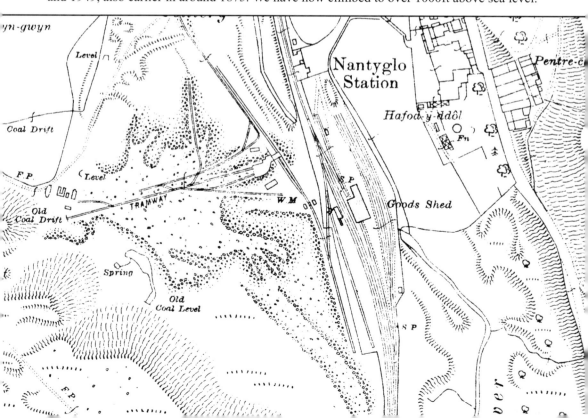

85.　　A southward view in July 1957 includes the well ventilated lamp room. This station was the terminus from 1859 to 1906. Traffic demanded eleven men here throughout the 1930s. (R.M.Casserley)

86.　　It is 24th July 1958 and token exchange is about to take place at the 20-lever signal box. Note that the passing loop was south of the platform. (G.Adams/ M.J.Stretton coll.)

87.　　The public goods yard was at the other side of the line and its gateway is seen in 1962 from the last train. Both passenger and local goods traffic ceased on 30th April 1962. For many years prior to the 1906 "Missing Link" to Brynmawr, the line continued north to Nantyglo Ironworks, from which there was a connection to Brynmawr. (Stations UK)

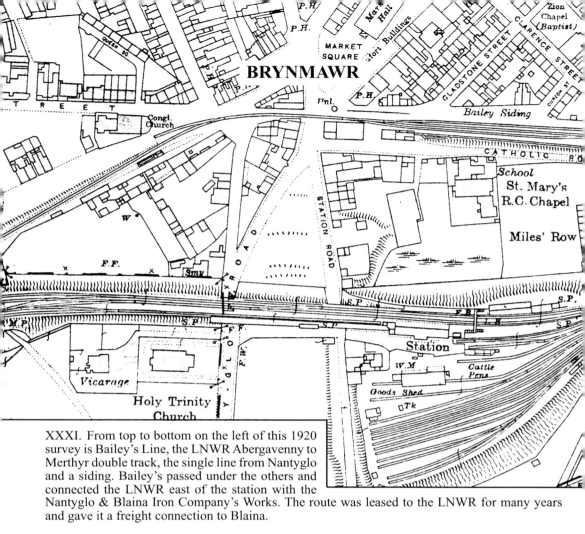

XXXI. From top to bottom on the left of this 1920 survey is Bailey's Line, the LNWR Abergavenny to Merthyr double track, the single line from Nantyglo and a siding. Bailey's passed under the others and connected the LNWR east of the station with the Nantyglo & Blaina Iron Company's Works. The route was leased to the LNWR for many years and gave it a freight connection to Blaina.

88.   In the foreground is the line from Nantyglo and in the background is the former LNWR No. 2 Box. The bridges are over the trackbed of Bailey's Line in this 1950s eastward view. The climb from Nantyglo was mostly at 1 in 54, but this final length was 1 in 47. The locomotive is standing on the run-round loop west of the station. Western Valleys trains usually reversed out of platform 4 for the loco to attach to the other end of the train and push it back into the platform. (W.J.Skillern/D.Edge coll.)

89. On the left is the bay platform for trains from Nantyglo. We look southwest from the ex-LNWR platform for trains from Merthyr. The 0-6-0PT is no. 8436 and was recorded in about 1957. (W.J.Skillern/ D.Edge coll.)

90. This is the east end of the station in 1951, with a train from Abergavenny arriving on the left. The route to Blaenavon is in the centre; this line lost its passenger service in 1941. No. 1 Box is included; it was built in 1915. (D.Edge coll.)

91. Pannier Tanks, such as this, had been a common sight on the joint line from Nantyglo; they were also used on the Abergavenny-Merthyr route after it was transferred to the Western Region at the end of 1948. This photograph is from 1957. All the Merthyr-Abergavenny trains were worked from the Merthyr end, after the closure of Abergavenny (former LNWR) shed in 1952. (G.Adams/M.J.Stretton coll.)

92.   This is the west end of the station in 1957, the right signal arm being for Nantyglo. The entrance to the station was on the southside. These signals also appear in the next picture. (H.C.Casserley)

Other views of this station can be found in
***Abergavenny to Merthyr* and**
***Monmouthshire Eastern Valleys*.**

93.   Platform 4 was for Nantyglo trains and was opened in 1906. Timber was used as it was constructed on the edge of an embankment. The photograph was taken in the last month of service, April 1962. The east-west trains had been withdrawn in January 1958, so this was the last platform in use. (D.K.Jones coll.)

Ebbw Vale Branch

MARINE COLLIERY PLATFORM

XXXII. The halt opened in 1890 and is at the top of this 1921 map, which has been reduced to 15ins to 1 mile. Closing that year was the 13-lever Marine Colliery Sidings box, which was later moved to Cwm station. Llandafal Colliery (right) closed in about 1922.

Marine Platform

Marine Colliery

Shaft

Coke Ovens

Shaft

Shaft

Old Air Shaft

Coal Level

Llan-dafal

Old Quarry

Weir

Marine Sidings

Engine House

Old Quarry

Ebbw River (Afon Ebwy)

Spring

Craig Fawr Sidings (see p. 85)

Spring

Spring

Tank

Spring

Tank

Old Shaft

Graig Fawr Colliery (Disused)

Tank

Old Coal Shaft

G.W.

94. The site was initially called Cwm Colliers Halt and is seen on the left, along with Cwm South box (26 levers), which functioned until 10th July 1968. Closing on the same day was Graig Fawr box (44 levers); this is at the bottom of the map. (D.Edge coll.)

95. At work at Marine Colliery on 4th April 1969 was NCB 0-4-0ST no. 31, a Peckett of 1917 named *Ebbw Vale* and much rebuilt using parts of two other similar locos. The colliery had opened in 1892 and belonged to the steelworks until nationalisation. (M.Dart)

96.   Passing the colliery with the OPC special the "Ebbw Vale" are nos. 37289 and 45055 *Royal Corp of Transport* on 18th September 1977. The line was singled on 31st July 1981. (P.Jones)

97.   Hunslet no. 7487 of 1976 was on duty on 26th September 1980. Coal production ceased here in August 1989. The 11-lever Cwm North box had been in the distance from 1891 until 1943, when Mon & Cwm Colliery closed. (D.H.Mitchell)

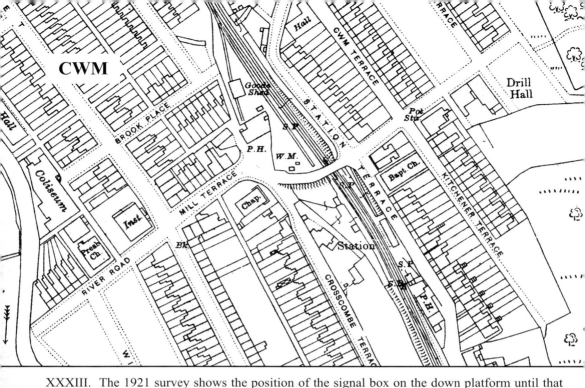

CWM

XXXIII. The 1921 survey shows the position of the signal box on the down platform until that time. A "new" one with 20 levers was built north of the top border, it functioning until 2nd July 1962. The goods yard was in use from 1915 to November 1963.

98.   A southward view in 1962 shows that the railway had been built on a shelf on the side of the valley. The line had been doubled in 1886. (Stations UK)

99. The SLS special on 6th May 1962 returns south behind 0-6-2T no. 6656. The station had at least 24 men on its payroll in the 1930s, most being engaged at the adjacent collieries. (D.Edge coll.)

100. Looking north from the road bridge on 8th May 1979, we witness the passage of the weedkiller train behind no. 25318. The goods yard had been on the left. (M.J.Hughes)

NORTH OF CWM

101. West of the main line was Waunllwyd Colliery sidings from 1903; they were on the east side until that time, but its spelling varied over the years. The owner was the Ebbw Vale Steel, Iron & Coal Co. Ltd, which explains the initials on the wagons. (D.Edge coll.)

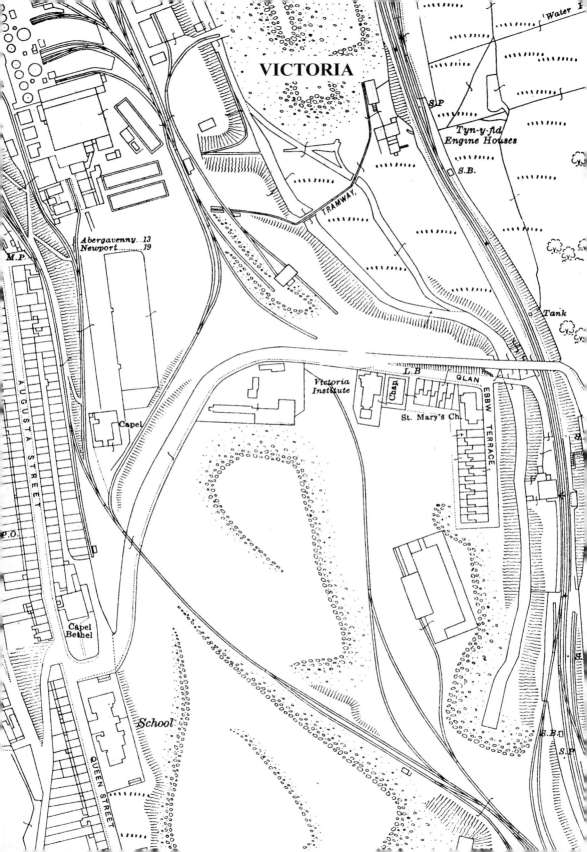

VICTORIA

Water

S.P

Tyn-y-fld
Engine Houses

S.B.

TRAMWAY

M.P.

Abergavenny...13
Newport........19

Tank

Victoria
Institute

L.B.

GLAN

Chap.

St. Mary's Ch.

EBBW

TERRACE

Capel

AUGUSTA STREET

P.O.

Capel
Bethel

School

QUEEN STREET

S.B.

S.P.

← XXXIV. Waunllwyd North box (20 levers) is lower right on this 1920 extract. It was replaced by a ground frame in September 1964. Victoria station is above it. At the top is Duffryn Sidings ground frame (S.B.), which was replaced by a signal box further north in 1939. This had 37 levers and was in use until September 1966. On the left is part of the Victoria Foundry complex.

102. A view southwards shows the post-1920 footbridge in 1962. Like Cwm, this station was listed from 1852. There were 18 employees here in 1929, mainly working on mineral traffic. (Stations UK)

103. No. 37887 was involved in major engineering works in May 1989. Map XXXIV shows the circuitous route taken by the A4046 north of the station. A new bridge allowed it to be diverted over the former slag tip sites on a near straight alignment. (M.J.Hughes)

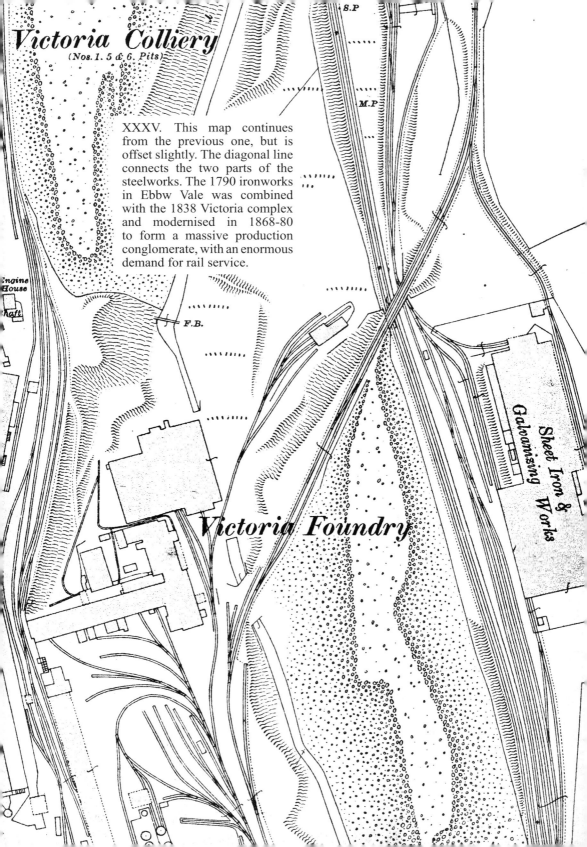

Victoria Colliery
(Nos. 1. 5 & 6. Pits)

XXXV. This map continues from the previous one, but is offset slightly. The diagonal line connects the two parts of the steelworks. The 1790 ironworks in Ebbw Vale was combined with the 1838 Victoria complex and modernised in 1868-80 to form a massive production conglomerate, with an enormous demand for rail service.

S.P

M.P

ngine
House

haft

F.B.

Victoria Foundry

Sheet Iron &
Galvanising
Works

TYLLWYN HALT

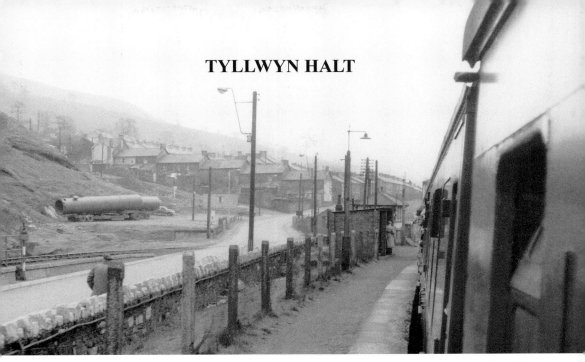

104.   The halt opened on 29th November 1943 and was situated near Ebbw Vale Sidings box, which is top right on the next map; "South" was dropped that day. It had a 38-lever frame and closed on 10th July 1968. This is the view south in 1962; the box is at the end of the platform. The double track ended here. (Stations UK)

105.   There was only one platform, as the line was bidirectional. The parallel track (right) was a works line. We are looking north at one of the many tips which scarred the area. There was also an up goods loop on the other side of the train. (Stations UK)

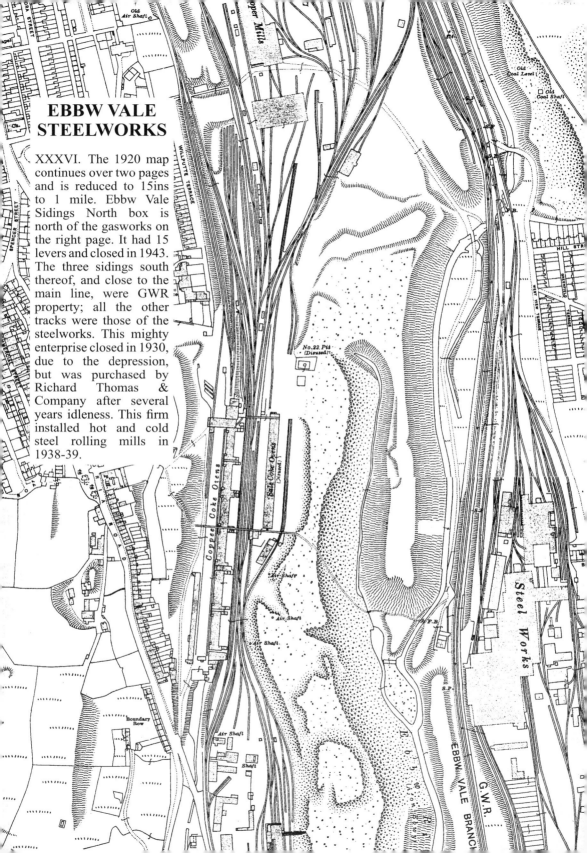

EBBW VALE STEELWORKS

XXXVI. The 1920 map continues over two pages and is reduced to 15ins to 1 mile. Ebbw Vale Sidings North box is north of the gasworks on the right page. It had 15 levers and closed in 1943. The three sidings south thereof, and close to the main line, were GWR property; all the other tracks were those of the steelworks. This mighty enterprise closed in 1930, due to the depression, but was purchased by Richard Thomas & Company after several years idleness. This firm installed hot and cold steel rolling mills in 1938-39.

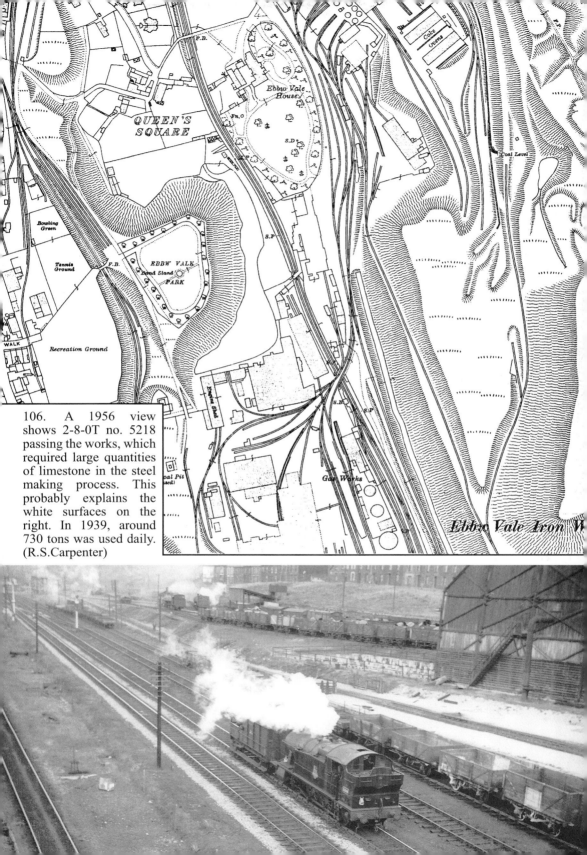

106. A 1956 view shows 2-8-0T no. 5218 passing the works, which required large quantities of limestone in the steel making process. This probably explains the white surfaces on the right. In 1939, around 730 tons was used daily. (R.S.Carpenter)

107. Initially iron ore was dug out between the coal seams in many areas, but latterly it was all imported. Another 1956 photograph and this includes a further load of ore arriving. There were four trains daily from Northamptonshire in the 1940s.
(P.Q.Treloar)

108. Poor visibility was common owing to pollution and mist due to altitude; the works was about 900ft above sea level. This photograph of 2-8-2T no. 7227 is included to remind us that other chemicals were required by the works.
(D.K.Jones coll.)

109. Drizzle was another feature of the impressive and extensive site. Robert Stephenson 0-6-0ST no. 54 wanders across the road in April 1962. The works had 57½ miles of track when completed.
(D.K.Jones coll.)

110. Sister engine no. 52 was set aside when pictured on 16th July 1963. The loco fleet was very extensive; back in 1938, there were 32 steam and one diesel listed. They were handling 0.5m tons of sheet steel and tinplate per annum. In the background are the fine 1915 offices, which still stand. (Rev. A.Newman/C.G.Maggs coll.)

111. The Lea Valley Railway Club's "Severn Chopper Express" visited this amazing site on 3rd September 1978, using nos 20156 and 20175. The works was 2½ miles long and ¾ mile wide. (K.Jones)

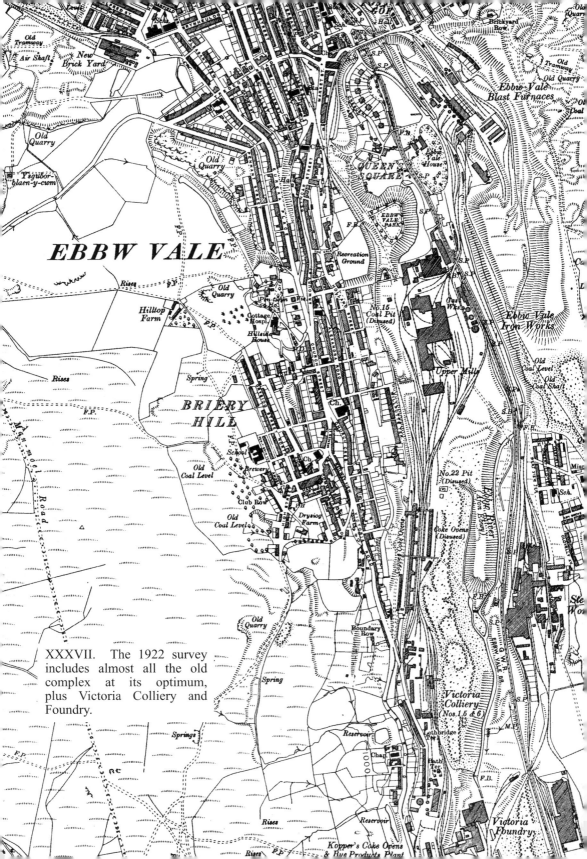

XXXVII. The 1922 survey includes almost all the old complex at its optimum, plus Victoria Colliery and Foundry.

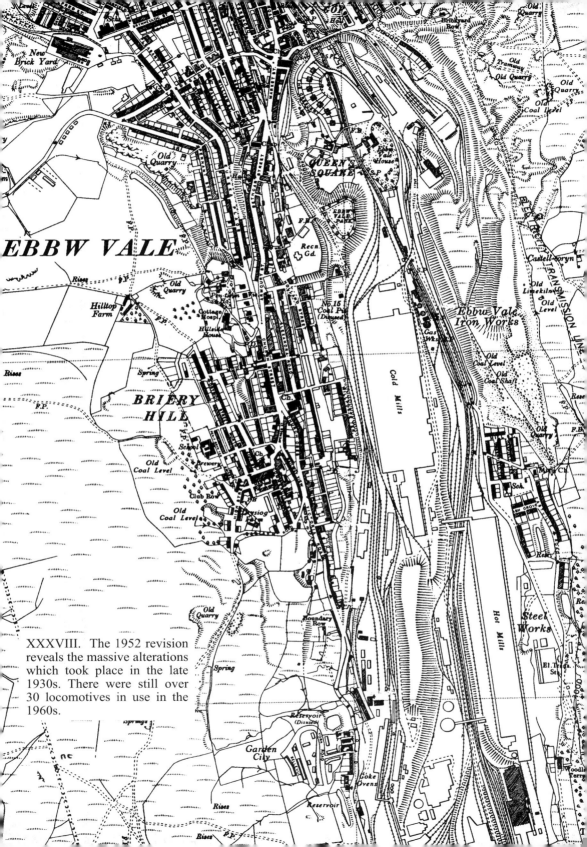

XXXVIII. The 1952 revision reveals the massive alterations which took place in the late 1930s. There were still over 30 locomotives in use in the 1960s.

112.   We now have two photographs from 8th September 1998. Here two of the works shunters are conveying wagons from the EWS sidings. They have climbed up the line in the foreground and then reversed. Steelmaking was slowly eliminated in the 1970s and so steel was brought in by rail from elsewhere. (D.H.Mitchell)

113.   Nos 37903 and 37901 pass South ground frame with the 16.11 service to Margam. Tinplate production ceased in February 2001 and the track remained idle. However, some clearance work took place in 2006 on the route from Newport and fresh rails put ready for installation. (D.H.Mitchell)

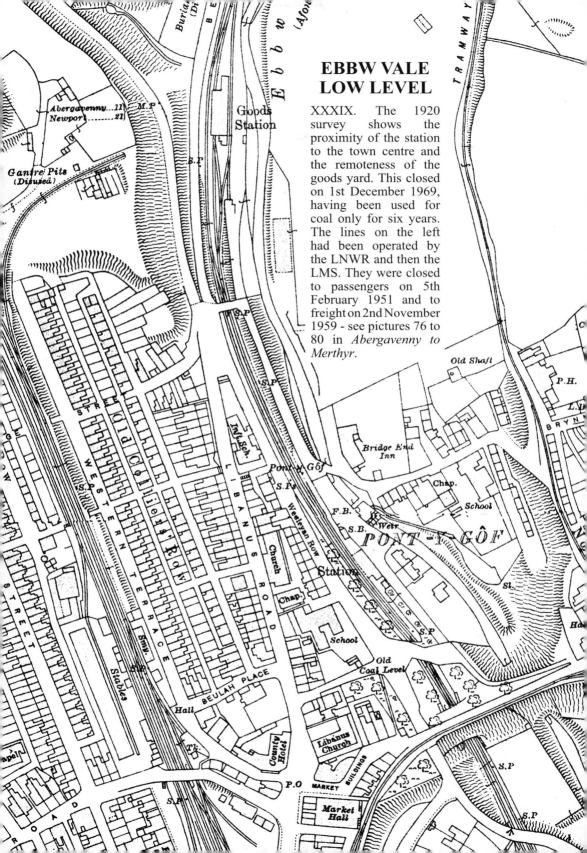

EBBW VALE LOW LEVEL

XXXIX. The 1920 survey shows the proximity of the station to the town centre and the remoteness of the goods yard. This closed on 1st December 1969, having been used for coal only for six years. The lines on the left had been operated by the LNWR and then the LMS. They were closed to passengers on 5th February 1951 and to freight on 2nd November 1959 - see pictures 76 to 80 in *Abergavenny to Merthyr*.

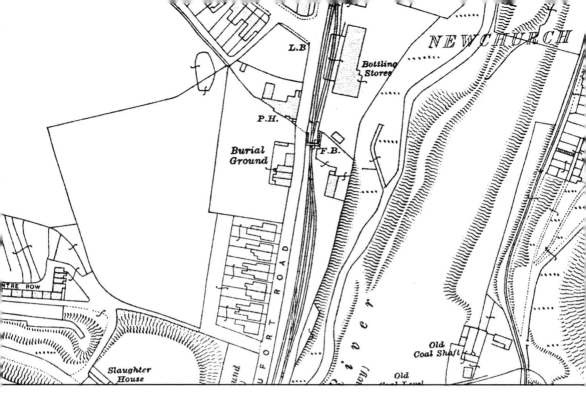

XL.   The line continued north to Beaufort for the conveyance of minerals and workmen, but there was no platform there. Miners trains were running by at least 1886 and a regular such service between there and Cwm was provided until October 1961. This map runs on from the top of the previous one and shows the 1910 siding for the Valleys Bottling & Mineral Waters Co. Ltd. It lasted until 1953, but serving other firms; the line northwards closed in 1962 and southwards in 1969.

114.   The general scene is set with the postcard panorama from the Edwardian era. It is a northward view from the bottom of the map. (D.Edge coll.)

115.　The staffing level was 44 in 1923 and 62 in 1937. Another postcard print in the same direction gives a close-up of the stone building and fine garden. (D.Edge coll.)

116.　The suffix "Low Level" was added by BR on 19th April 1952. The station had been completely rebuilt in brick and more than doubled in length. The short train has just arrived behind an 0-6-2T. (P.Q.Treloar)

117.   No. 6415 is ready to depart for Aberbeeg at 6.20pm on 26th May 1956. There was an electric train staff for the single line to Ebbw Vale Sidings box and a wooden staff for the route to Beaufort. (F.Hornby)

118.   This photograph from 12th July 1958 serves as a reminder of the high rainfall in the area. The 9.15am departure would be hauled by 0-6-0PT no. 3798; it is about to run round its train. (H.C.Casserley)

90

89

88

87

86

85

84

83

82

81

80

79

78

77

76

75

74

73

35'

30'

A 467
Risca
3 miles

A 468
Caerphilly
9 miles

A 4072

A 48 (T)
Cardiff
8 miles

CARDIFF

B 4239

Wentlooge

Coed
Garw

Gwastad-
mawr

Ynys-y-
Fro Res

Allt-yr-yn

Crindau

Locks

Sch

Christchurch

LANGSTONE

Maindee

St. Julian's
Wood
Cem

Pen-y-Lan

Fourteen
Locks

High
Cross

Gold
Tops

Castle

Ladi Hill

Kingsland
Top

Milton

Llan-wern

Bishpool

Llanwern

Golf Course

CH

The Barn

Lis-werry

NEWPORT

Port par

Basaleg Junc Sta

Pye
Corner

Stelvio

CH

Sch

Tredegar
Camp

Golf
Course

Pillgwenlly

Level of
Mendalgyf

Transporter

Pylons

B 4237

Upper Lake

Tube Works

Brass
Gout

Pont-
Ebbw

Maes-glas

Traston

Lower Lake

Tatton Fm

New Ho

Tredegar House

South Dock

Dry
Dock

Moorbarn

Pye
Corner

Broadstreet Common

Great
Newra

Green
Court

Whitson Court

Tredegar
Park

DUFFRYN

Pen-carn

Julian's
Gout

Burnt
Ho

Henton
Fm

Whitson
Common

Great
Pen-carn
Reen

Fair
Orchard

New
Gout

Pen

RIVER USK

Nash

Moorlands

Goldcliff

Percoed
Reen

St BRIDE'S WENTLOOG

New House

Level Court
Saltmarsh

Inn

Clifton
Court

St Bride's
Wentlooge

Farmfield

Priory
(Remains of)

Gold

Hawse
Fm

Reen

Breakwater

Orchard
Fm

Level

Sealand

Sutton
Inn

U s k

P a t c h

Welsh

Hook

MIDDLE

OF

GROUNDS

THE

Lightship

M

119.   DMUs became the norm in 1958; this one is seen in 1961. The line south of the station to the steelworks closed in 1975, singling having taken place in 1964. Only the station house remained standing. (R.E.Toop)

120.   The signal box had 46 levers and closed on 17th August 1964. A gloomy day in 1962 is an appropriate end to our visit to the Western Valleys. (D.Lawrence)

MP Middleton Press

EVOLVING THE ULTIMATE RAIL ENCYCLOPEDIA

Easebourne Lane, Midhurst, West Sussex.
GU29 9AZ   Tel:01730 813169

www.middletonpress.co.uk   email:info@middletonpress.co.uk

A-0 906520   B-1 873793   C-1 901706   D-1 904474

OOP Out of Print at time of printing - Please check current availability   **BROCHURE AVAILABLE SHOWING NEW TITLES**

A
Abergavenny to Merthyr C 91 5
Aldgate & Stepney Tramways B 70 7
Allhallows - Branch Line to A 62 2
Alton - Branch Lines to A 11 8
Andover to Southampton A 82 7
Ascot - Branch Lines around A 64 9
Ashburton - Branch Line to B 95 2
Ashford - Steam to Eurostar B 67 7
Ashford to Dover A 48 7
Austrian Narrow Gauge D 04 7
Avonmouth - BL around D 42 X

B
Banbury to Birmingham D 27 6
Barnet & Finchley Tramways B 93 6
Barry - Branch Lines around D 50 0
Basingstoke to Salisbury A 89 4
Bath Green Park to Bristol C 36 2
Bath to Evercreech Junction A 60 6
Bath Tramways B 86 3
Battle over Portsmouth 1940 A 29 0
Battle over Sussex 1940 A 79 7
Bedford to Wellingborough D 31 4
Betwixt Petersfield & Midhurst A 94 0
Blitz over Sussex 1941-42 B 35 9
Bognor at War 1939-45 B 59 6
Bombers over Sussex 1943-45 B 51 0
Bournemouth & Poole Trys B 47 2
Bournemouth to Evercreech Jn A 46 0
Bournemouth to Weymouth A 57 6
Bournemouth Trolleybuses C 10 9
Bradford Trolleybuses D 19 5
Brecon to Neath D 43 8
Brecon to Newport D 16 0
Brickmaking in Sussex B 19 7
Brightons Tramways B 02 2 OOP
Brighton to Eastbourne A 16 9
Brighton to Worthing A 03 7
Brighton Trolleybuses D 34 9
Bristols Tramways B 57 X
Bristol to Taunton D 03 9
Bromley South to Rochester B 23 5
Bromsgrove to Gloucester D 73 X
Brunel - A railtour of his achievements D 74 8
Bude - Branch Line to B 29 4
Burnham to Evercreech Jn A 68 1
Burton & Ashby Tramways C 51 6

C
Camberwell & West Norwood Tys B 22 7
Cambridge to Ely D 55 1
Canterbury - Branch Lines around B 58 8
Cardiff Trolleybuses D 64 0
Caterham & Tattenham Corner B 25 1
Changing Midhurst C 15 X
Chard and Yeovil - BLs around C 30 3
Charing Cross to Dartford A 75 4
Charing Cross to Orpington A 96 7
Cheddar - Branch Line to B 90 1
Cheltenham to Andover C 43 5
Cheltenham to Redditch B 81 0
Chesterfield Tramways C 37 3
Chesterfield Trolleybuses D 51 9
Chichester to Portsmouth A 14 2
Clapham & Streatham Trys B 97 9 OOP
Clapham Junction - 50 yrs C 06 0 OOP
Clapham Junction to Beckenham Jn B 36 7
Clevedon & Portishead - BLs to D 18 7
Collectors Trains, Trolleys & Trams D 29 2
Colonel Stephens D62 4
Cornwall Narrow Gauge D 56 X
Crawley to Littlehampton A 34 7
Cromer - Branch Lines around C 26 5
Croydons Tramways B 42 1
Croydons Trolleybuses B 73 1 OOP
Croydon to East Grinstead B 48 0
Crystal Palace (HL) & Catford Loop A 87 8

D
Darlington Trolleybuses D 33 0
Dartford to Sittingbourne B 34 0
Derby Tramways D 17 9
Derby Trolleybuses C 72 9
Derwent Valley - Branch Line to the D 06 3
Didcot to Banbury D 02 0
Didcot to Swindon C 84 2
Didcot to Winchester C 13 3
Dorset & Somerset Narrow Gauge D 76 4
Douglas to Peel C 88 5
Douglas to Port Erin C 55 9
Douglas to Ramsey D 39 X
Dovers Tramways B 24 3
Dover to Ramsgate A 78 9

E
Ealing to Slough C 42 7
Eastbourne to Hastings A 27 4
East Cornwall Mineral Railways D 22 5
East Croydon to Three Bridges A 53 3
East Grinstead - Branch Lines to A 07 X
East Ham & West Ham Tramways B 52 9
East Kent Light Railway A 61 4 OOP
East London - Branch Lines of C 44 3
East London Line B 80 4
East Ridings Secret Resistance D 21 7
Edgware & Willesden Tramways C 18 4
Effingham Junction - BLs around A 74 6
Eltham & Woolwich Tramways B 74 X OOP
Ely to Kings Lynn C 53 2
Ely to Norwich C 90 7
Embankment & Waterloo Tramways B 41 3
Enfield & Wood Green Trys C 03 6 OOP
Enfield Town & Palace Gates - BL to D 32 2
Epsom to Horsham A 30 4
Euston to Harrow & Wealdstone C 89 3
Exeter & Taunton Tramways B 32 4
Exeter to Newton Abbot C 49 4
Exeter to Tavistock B 69 3
Exmouth - Branch Lines to B 00 6

F
Fairford - Branch Line to A 52 5
Falmouth, Helston & St. Ives - BL to C 74 5
Fareham to Salisbury A 67 3
Faversham to Dover B 05 7
Felixstowe & Aldeburgh - BL to D 20 9
Fenchurch Street to Barking C 20 6
Festiniog - 50 yrs of enterprise C 83 4
Festiniog in the Fifties B 68 5
Festiniog in the Sixties B 91 X
Finsbury Park to Alexandra Palace C 02 8
Frome to Bristol B 77 4
Fulwell - Trams, Trolleys & Buses D 11 X

G
Gloucester to Bristol D 35 7
Gloucester to Cardiff D 66 7
Gosport & Horndean Trys B 92 8
Gosport - Branch Lines around A 36 3
Great Yarmouth Tramways D 13 6
Greece Narrow Gauge D 72 1
Greenwich & Dartford Tramways B 14 6 OOP
Guildford to Redhill A 63 0

H
Hammersmith & Hounslow Trys C 33 8
Hampshire Narrow Gauge D 36 5
Hampshire Waterways A 84 3 OOP
Hampstead & Highgate Tramways B 53 7
Harrow to Watford D 14 4
Hastings to Ashford A 37 1 OOP
Hastings Tramways B 18 9
Hastings Trolleybuses B 81 2 OOP
Hawkhurst - Branch Line to A 66 5
Hayling - Branch Line to A 12 6
Haywards Heath to Seaford A 28 2
Henley, Windsor & Marlow - BL to C77 X
Hereford to Newport D 74 3
Horsham - Branch Lines to A 02 9
Huddersfield Trolleybuses C 92 3
Hull Tramways D60 8
Hull Trolleybuses D 24 1
Huntingdon - Branch Lines around A 93 2

I
Ilford & Barking Tramways B 61 8
Ilford to Shenfield C 97 4
Ilfracombe - Branch Line to B 21 9
Ilkeston & Glossop Tramways D 40 3
Industrial Rlys of the South East A 09 6
Ipswich to Saxmundham C 41 9
Ipswich Trolleybuses D 59 4
Isle of Wight Lines - 50 yrs C 12 5

K
Kent & East Sussex Waterways A 72 X
Kent Narrow Gauge C 45 1
Kent Seaways - Hoys to Hovercraft D 79 9
Kingsbridge - Branch Line to C 98 2
Kingston & Hounslow Loops A83 5 OOP
Kingston & Wimbledon Tramways B 56 1
Kingswear - Branch Line to C 17 6

L
Lambourn - Branch Line to C 70 2
Launceston & Princetown - BL to C 19 2
Lewisham & Catford Tramways B 26 X OOP
Lewisham to Dartford A 92 4

Lines around Wimbledon B 75 8
Liverpool Street to Chingford D 01 2
Liverpool Street to Ilford C 34 6
Liverpool Tramways - Eastern C 04 4
Liverpool Tramways - Northern C 46 X
Liverpool Tramways - Southern C 23 0
London Bridge to Addiscombe B 20 0
London Bridge to East Croydon A 58 4
London Chatham & Dover Railway A 88 6
London Termini - Past and Proposed D 00 4
London to Portsmouth Waterways B 43 X
Longmoor - Branch Line to A 41 X
Looe - Branch Line to C 22 2
Lyme Regis - Branch Line to A 45 2
Lynton - Branch Line to B 04 9

M
Maidstone & Chatham Tramways B 40 5
Maidstone Trolleybuses C 00 1 OOP
March - Branch Lines around B 09 X
Margate & Ramsgate Tramways C 52 4
Marylebone to Rickmansworth D49 7
Midhurst - Branch Lines around A 49 5
Midhurst - Branch Lines to A 01 0 OOP
Military Defence of West Sussex A 23 1
Military Signals, South Coast C 54 0
Minehead - Branch Line to A 80 0
Mitcham Junction Lines B 01 4
Mitchell & company C 59 1
Monmouthshire Eastern Valleys D 71 3
Moreton-in-Marsh to Worcester D 26 8
Moretonhampstead - BL to C 27 3
Mountain Ash to Neath D 80 2

N
Newbury to Westbury C 66 4
Newcastle to Hexham D 69 1
Newcastle Trolleybuses D 78 0
Newport (IOW) - Branch Lines to A 26 6
Newquay - Branch Lines to C 71 0
Newton Abbot to Plymouth C 60 5
Northern France Narrow Gauge C 75 3
North East German Narrow Gauge D 44 6
North Kent Tramways B 44 8
North London Line B 94 4
North Woolwich - BLs around C 65 6
Norwich Tramways C 40 0
Nottinghamshire & Derbyshire T/B D 63 2
Nottinghamshire & Derbyshire T/W D 53 5

O
Orpington to Tonbridge B 03 0 OOP
Oxford to Bletchley D57 8
Oxford to Moreton-in-Marsh D 15 2

P
Paddington to Ealing C 37 0
Paddington to Princes Risborough C 81 8
Padstow - Branch Line to B 54 5
Plymouth - BLs around B 98 7
Plymouth to St. Austell C 63 X
Pontypool to Mountain Ash D 65 9
Porthmadog 1954-94 - BL around B 31 6
Porthmadog to Blaenau B 50 2 OOP
Portmadoc 1923-46 - BL around B 13 8
Portsmouths Tramways B 72 3
Portsmouth to Southampton A 31 2
Portsmouth Trolleybuses C 73 7
Potters Bar to Cambridge D 70 5
Princes Risborough - Branch Lines to D 05 5
Princes Risborough to Banbury C 85 0

R
Railways to Victory C 16 8/7 OOP
Reading to Basingstoke B 27 8
Reading to Didcot C 79 6
Reading to Guildford A 47 9 OOP
Reading Tramways B 87 1
Reading Trolleybuses C 05 2
Redhill to Ashford A 73 8
Return to Blaenau 1970-82 C 64 8
Rickmansworth to Aylesbury D 61 6
Roman Roads of Hampshire D 67 5
Roman Roads of Surrey C 61 3
Roman Roads of Sussex C 48 6
Romneyrail C 32 X
Ryde to Ventnor A 19 3

S
Salisbury to Westbury B 39 1
Salisbury to Yeovil B 06 5 OOP
Saxmundham to Yarmouth C 69 9
Saxony Narrow Gauge D 47 0
Seaton & Eastbourne Tramways B 76 6 OOP
Seaton & Sidmouth - Branch Lines to A 95 9
Secret Sussex Resistance B 82 0
SECR Centenary album C 11 7
Selsey - Branch Line to A 04 5
Sheerness - Branch Lines around B 16 2

Shepherds Bush to Uxbridge T/Ws C
Shrewsbury - Branch Line to A 86 X
Sierra Leone Narrow Gauge D 28 4
Sittingbourne to Ramsgate A 90 8
Slough to Newbury C 56 7
Solent - Creeks, Crafts & Cargoes D 7
Southamptons Tramways B 33 2
Southampton to Bournemouth A 42 1
Southend-on-Sea Tramways B 28 6
Southern France Narrow Gauge C 4
Southwark & Deptford Tramways B
Southwold - Branch Line to A 15 0
South Eastern & Chatham Railways
South London Line B 46 4
South London Tramways 1903-33 D
St. Albans to Bedford D 08 X
St. Austell to Penzance C 67 2
St. Pancras to Barking D 68 3
St. Pancras to St. Albans C 78 8
Stamford Hill Tramways B 85 5
Steaming through Cornwall B 30 8 C
Steaming through Kent A 13 4 OOP
Steaming through the Isle of Wight A
Steaming through West Hants A 69 X
Stratford upon Avon to Birmingham
Stratford upon Avon to Cheltenham
Strood to Paddock Wood B 12 X
Surrey Home Guard C 57 5
Surrey Narrow Gauge C 87 7
Surrey Waterways A 51 7 OOP
Sussex Home Guard C 24 9
Sussex Narrow Gauge C 68 0
Sussex Shipping Sail, Steam & Moto
Swanley to Ashford B 45 6
Swindon to Bristol C 96 6
Swindon to Gloucester D46 2
Swindon to Newport D 30 6
Swiss Narrow Gauge C 94 X

T
Talyllyn - 50 years C 39 7
Taunton to Barnstaple B 60 X
Taunton to Exeter C 82 6
Tavistock to Plymouth B 88 X
Tees-side Trolleybuses D 58 6
Tenterden - Branch Line to A 21 5
Thanet's Tramways B 11 1 OOP
Three Bridges to Brighton A 35 5
Tilbury Loop C 86 9
Tiverton - Branch Lines around C 62
Tivetshall to Beccles D 41 1
Tonbridge to Hastings A 44 4
Torrington - Branch Lines to B 37 5
Tunbridge Wells - Branch Lines to A
Twickenham & Kingston Trys C 35
Two-Foot Gauge Survivors C 21 4 O

U
Upwell - Branch Line to B 64 2

V
Victoria & Lambeth Tramways B 49
Victoria to Bromley South A 98 3
Victoria to East Croydon A 40 1 OO
Vivarais C 31 1

W
Walthamstow & Leyton Tramways
Waltham Cross & Edmonton Trys C
Wandsworth & Battersea Tramways
Wantage - Branch Line to D 25 X
Wareham to Swanage - 50 yrs D 09 8
War on the Line A 10 X
War on the Line VIDEO + 88 0
Waterloo to Windsor A 54 1
Waterloo to Woking A 38 X
Watford to Leighton Buzzard D 45 4
Wenford Bridge to Fowey C 09 5
Westbury to Bath B 55 3
Westbury to Taunton C 76 1
West Cornwall Mineral Railways D
West Croydon to Epsom B 08 1
West London - Branch Lines of C 50
West London Line B 84 7
West Sussex Waterways A 24 X OOP
West Wiltshire - Branch Lines of D 1
Weymouth - Branch Lines around A
Willesden Junction to Richmond B 7
Wimbledon to Beckenham C 58 3
Wimbledon to Epsom B 62 6
Wimborne - Branch Lines around A
Wisbech - Branch Lines around C 0
Wisbech 1800-1901 C 93 1
Woking to Alton A 59 2
Woking to Portsmouth A 25 8
Woking to Southampton A 55 X
Woolwich & Dartford Trolleys B 66
Worcester to Hereford D 38 1
Worthing to Chichester A 06 1

Y
Yeovil - 50 yrs change C 38 9
Yeovil to Dorchester A 76 2 OOP
Yeovil to Exeter A 91 6
York Tramways & Trolleybuses D 82